"Iain Duguid's *Turning the World Upside Down*—based on the opening chapters of Acts—is a splendid gift to us from a writer who stands in the church's best tradition of being both a professor and pastor. It skillfully combines faithful interpretation of Scripture with clear and relevant applications. It is scholarly yet readable, simple yet enriching, enjoyable yet challenging, packed with expositions of the 'there and then' that help us see and feel their implications for the 'here and now.' Here is a book to help both the church and the individual Christian turn our world 'upside down' in order to turn it 'the right way up.'"

Sinclair B. Ferguson, Chancellor's Professor of Systematic Theology, Reformed Theological Seminary; Teaching Fellow, Ligonier Ministries

"Though undergirded by Iain Duguid's profound scriptural knowledge, *Turning the World Upside Down* is not a dense theological treatise on the important New Testament book of Acts. Rather, it walks through the story told in the first eight chapters, presenting its profound truths in a conversational way, making penetrating and personal applications at every step."

Nancy Guthrie, author, *Saved: Experiencing the Promise of the Book of Acts*

"My colleague, friend, and former pastor Iain Duguid has dedicated his life to understanding the Scriptures at their full depth, teaching biblical truths in an understandable way, and growing healthy churches by developing godly leaders. This makes him the ideal pastor to do what he does so helpfully in *Turning the World Upside Down*: connect the story of the first church to the ministry needs and gospel opportunities of the church in today's post-Christian, prerevival society."

Philip Graham Ryken, President, Wheaton College

"One suspects that Iain Duguid's *Turning the World Upside Down* is meant to help turn the church right side up. Local church leaders and church 'starter-uppers' could get their sea legs here (don't miss, by the way, the superb treatment of Acts 2:42–47). More broadly, Duguid's exposition carries just the right balance of bite and comfort; yet the reader has the strange sense that he or she is being 'chased,' for Iain repeatedly and relentlessly pursues the religious and the raunchy, the respectable and the rebellious, with the claims of the upside-down gospel."

Dale Ralph Davis, former Professor of Old Testament, Reformed Theological Seminary, Jackson

"Iain Duguid's combined experience as a biblical scholar, church planter, and preacher makes *Turning the World Upside Down* a practical, illuminating, and challenging exploration of the achievement of the risen Lord Jesus through the Holy Spirit in the infancy of the church in its new covenant form. Duguid shows from the early chapters of Acts that both the planting and the thriving of churches are attributable not to our methods but to the sovereign power and presence of Christ himself—a message that both pastors and God's people must take to heart."

Dennis E. Johnson, Professor Emeritus of Practical Theology, Westminster Seminary California; author, *The Message of Acts in the History of Redemption*; *Let's Study Acts*; and *Perfect Priest for Weary Pilgrims*

"Warm and wise, clear and edifying—this is a wonderful exposition of Acts 1–8 from a seasoned pastor and professor. Iain Duguid skillfully relates the teaching of Acts to the rest of Scripture, and to our lives today."

Brandon D. Crowe, Professor of New Testament, Westminster Theological Seminary

"At a time when it seems like Christianity is fading in the West, Iain Duguid turns our focus to the explosive spread of the gospel in Acts. Ours is the God of the resurrection and Pentecost; bringing life out of death is his specialty. If you need a powerful dose of encouragement from the apostolic mission for your ministry and life in the church today, read this book!"

Michael Horton, J. Gresham Machen Professor of Systematic Theology and Apologetics, Westminster Seminary California

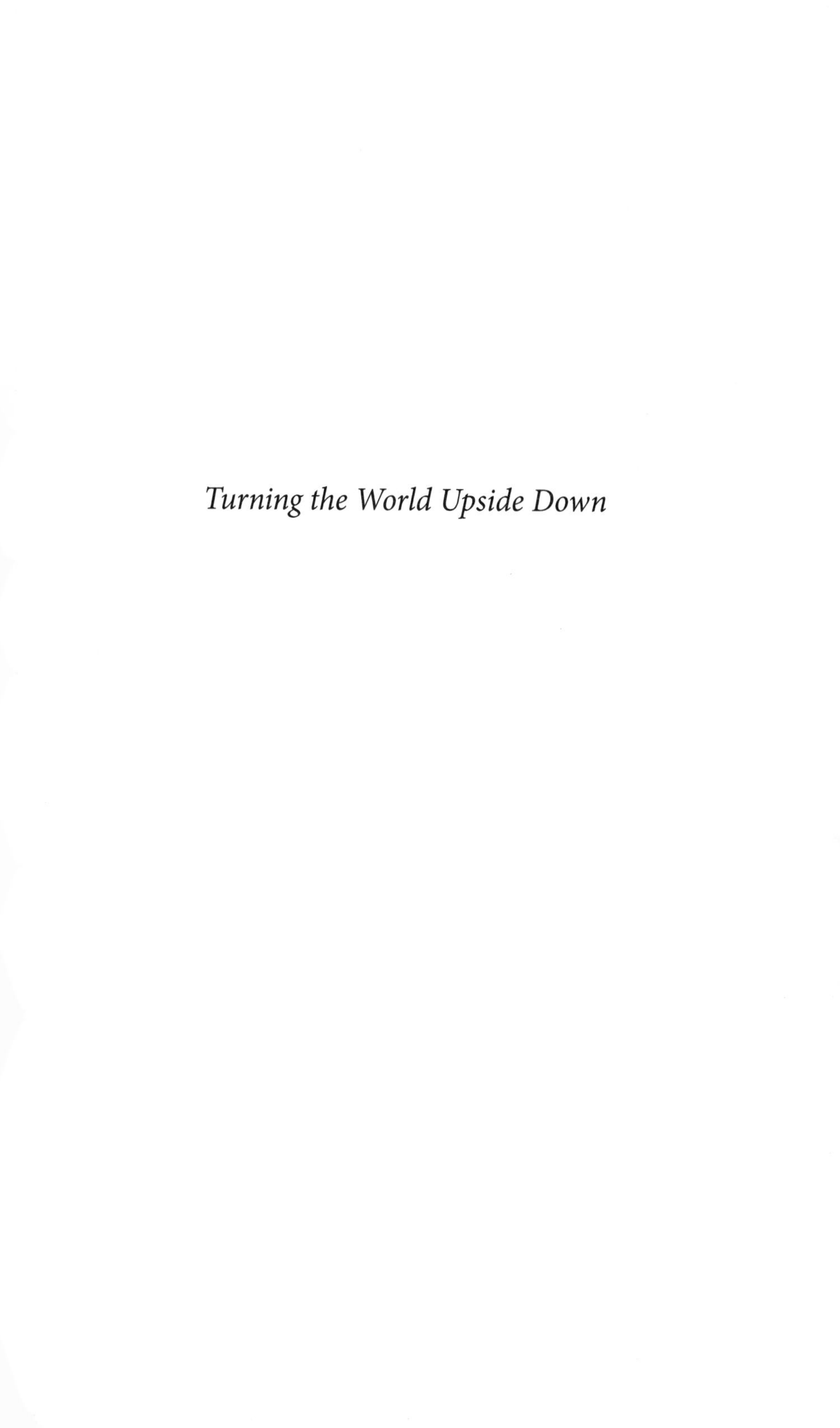

Turning the World Upside Down

Crossway Books by Iain M. Duguid

Numbers: God's Presence in the Wilderness

The Whole Armor of God: How Christ's Victory Strengthens Us for Spiritual Warfare

Turning the World Upside Down

Lessons for the Church from Acts 1–8

Iain M. Duguid

WHEATON, ILLINOIS

Turning the World Upside Down: Lessons for the Church from Acts 1–8

© 2025 by Iain M. Duguid

Published by Crossway
1300 Crescent Street
Wheaton, Illinois 60187

All rights reserved. No part of this publication may be reproduced, stored in a retrieval system, or transmitted in any form by any means, electronic, mechanical, photocopy, recording, or otherwise, without the prior permission of the publisher, except as provided for by USA copyright law. Crossway® is a registered trademark in the United States of America.

Cover design: David Fassett

Cover image: Rawpixel

First printing 2025

Printed in the United States of America

Unless otherwise indicated, Scripture quotations are from the ESV® Bible (The Holy Bible, English Standard Version®), © 2001 by Crossway, a publishing ministry of Good News Publishers. Used by permission. All rights reserved. The ESV text may not be quoted in any publication made available to the public by a Creative Commons license. The ESV may not be translated in whole or in part into any other language.

Scripture quotations marked NIV are taken from the Holy Bible, New International Version®, NIV®. Copyright © 1973, 1978, 1984, 2011 by Biblica, Inc.™ Used by permission of Zondervan. All rights reserved worldwide. www.zondervan.com. The "NIV" and "New International Version" are trademarks registered in the United States Patent and Trademark Office by Biblica, Inc.™

All emphases in Scripture quotations have been added by the author.

Trade Paperback ISBN: 978-1-4335-9896-8
ePub ISBN: 978-1-4335-9898-2
PDF ISBN: 978-1-4335-9897-5

Library of Congress Cataloging-in-Publication Data

Names: Duguid, Iain M., author.
Title: Turning the world upside down : lessons for the church from Acts 1–8 / Iain M. Duguid.
Description: Wheaton, Illinois : Crossway, 2025. | Includes bibliographical references and index.
Identifiers: LCCN 2024029647 (print) | LCCN 2024029648 (ebook) | ISBN 9781433598968 (trade paperback) | ISBN 9781433598975 (pdf) | ISBN 9781433598982 (epub)
Subjects: LCSH: Bible. Acts—Criticism, interpretation, etc. | Church history—Primitive and early church, ca. 30-600.
Classification: LCC BS2635.52 .D84 2025 (print) | LCC BS2635.52 (ebook) | DDC 226/.06—dc23/eng/20250107
LC record available at https://lccn.loc.gov/2024029647
LC ebook record available at https://lccn.loc.gov/2024029648

Crossway is a publishing ministry of Good News Publishers.

BP 33 32 31 30 29 28 27 26 25
14 13 12 11 10 9 8 7 6 5 4 3 2 1

In every church I have pastored, there has been a Barnabas or two, a son (or daughter) of encouragement (Acts 4:36), who helped Barb and me persevere when the going got tough. You know who you are, and I am profoundly grateful to God for you.

Contents

Acknowledgments

THE MATERIAL IN THIS BOOK has a long prehistory. I first preached through Acts in our tiny church plant on a low-income housing estate in Oxford, England, in 1993–1994. The centrality of the gospel in Luke's narrative of the early church gripped me then, and so I have preached through these same passages in all the churches I have pastored: in Fallbrook, California; Grove City, Pennsylvania; and Philadelphia, Pennsylvania. Each time I have returned to this part of the Bible, I have been encouraged and challenged by Luke's description not only of the early church that turned the world upside down (Acts 17:6) but of the continued work of Jesus through the Holy Spirit (see 1:1). By his power, Jesus maintained these sometimes small and often fragile communities in their faith, in spite of great persecution.

In each of these various settings, I have had people who went out of their way to support me in the challenges of ministry. Chief of these, of course, are my wife, Barb, and my children, all of whom heard on several occasions the sermons on which this book is based. Barb frequently suggested valuable improvements, though she is not responsible for the remaining faults. In addition, in each place, the Lord gave us people like Barnabas, the "son of encouragement" (Acts 4:36), who were never-flagging champions and supporters, even when times got hard. I could not have kept going without you, ministering the Spirit's encouragement to me in human form, week after week. Thank you all so much!

1

Mission Earth

Acts 1:1–11

OLD GRAVEYARDS are fascinating places. As you wander around them, you can read the epitaphs of people who died long ago. Some of those epitaphs are memorable. Alexander the Great's tomb reads, "A tomb now suffices him for whom the world was not enough." Winston Churchill's epitaph is, "I am ready to meet my Maker; whether my Maker is prepared for the ordeal of meeting me is another matter." An old tombstone belonging to a man named William Hahn simply says, "I told you I was sick!" For most people buried in an old graveyard, their epitaph is all that remains of them: Everything they turned their hand to during their lives has long since disintegrated into the dust. Here and there some people have made a lasting impression in the world—an Alexander or a Churchill. They wrote great books or influenced history or even founded a new religion. But they all, the greatest and the least, ended up in the graveyard, their life's work finished. They may have left behind them an epitaph or a monument to keep their memory alive, but that is all. They are no more.[1]

1 The first epitaph can be found in Jon R. Stone, *The Routledge Dictionary of Latin Quotations: The Illiterati's Guide to Latin Maxims, Mottoes, Proverbs, and Sayings* (Routledge, 2004), 334; the second in Gertrude Himmelfarb, *The Moral Imagination: From Adam Smith to Lionel Trilling*, 2nd ed. (Rowman & Littlefield, 2012), 252; the third in Richard F. Veit

The graveyard points us to one of the main differences between Christianity and every other religion. Unlike every other religion, Christianity's founder is still alive and active in the world, a point that the writer of the book of Acts wants to make clear at the outset. Buddha died; his teachings are left behind as a memorial to his greatness, but he is no longer active in the world. Mohammed died; his ideas are still revered by millions of people, but he himself is not involved in the spread of his religion. Not so with Christianity. We don't follow a religion based on the teachings of a great man who lived and died a long time ago. Jesus died *and rose again*, showing himself alive to his disciples with many convincing proofs (Acts 1:3). We are part of a movement that was begun by Jesus while he was still on earth and is continued by Jesus now from his exalted throne in heaven.

The Acts of the Risen Jesus

This is one of the central thrusts of the book of Acts. For a long time, this book has been called "The Acts of the Apostles," but it could equally well be called "The Acts of the Risen Jesus through the Holy Spirit," for it is every bit as much about what Jesus is doing in the world as what the apostles do. In the introduction to the book, the writer, Luke, refers to his former book, his Gospel, in which he "dealt with all that Jesus *began* to do and teach, until the day" of his ascension (Acts 1:1–2). This book, however, is about the events that follow, the continuing work of Jesus from heaven, through the Holy Spirit working in the apostles and the early church. This book is thus the first chapter of the working out of the promise of Jesus in Matthew 28:20: "I am with you always, to the end of the age." The book of Acts is primarily a record of what God is up to, not of the acts of the human actors who appear on his stage.

Luke opens his account by introducing readers to his audience, whom he describes as "Theophilus" (Acts 1:1). "Theophilus" may, of course, denote a particular historical individual to whom the work was

---

and Mark Nonestied, *New Jersey Cemeteries and Tombstones: History in the Landscape* (Rutgers University Press, 2008), 256.

dedicated, but we shouldn't miss the meaning of his name: "lover of God." Luke's goal in writing this book is to create a multitude of "lovers of God." Through the gospel declared on its pages, we see many being converted from *theomachoi* ("God fighters"; see 5:39) to *theophiloi* ("God lovers").[2] And Luke wants that group to include us.

In the first chapter of the book, during the transitional period between his resurrection and his ascension into heaven, we find Jesus involved in one central task, that of teaching the disciples, especially about the kingdom of God.[3] In this passage, we are going to see four things about Jesus's teaching during this period: (1) the simple fact *that* Jesus teaches the disciples, (2) the fact that Jesus very much *needs* to teach them, (3) the *content* of what Jesus teaches the disciples, and (4) the *goal* of Jesus's teaching.

Jesus Teaches His Disciples

First we note the simple fact that Jesus uses his final days on earth to teach his disciples. In an age like ours in which we are tripping over ourselves with enthusiasm to get out and do things—something, anything—it is good for us to be reminded that the first instruction Jesus gives to his followers is to wait: "Do not leave Jerusalem, but wait for the gift my Father promised" (Acts 1:4 NIV). Before they can begin their task of taking the message of Jesus Christ to the world, they first have to be instructed about that task and then be empowered for it.

There's an application here for our task of taking the good news to our own context. At the outset, it is crucial to be sure that we are as clear as possible about what our task involves and to remind ourselves at every step of our dependence on the Holy Spirit in that task. We need a clear vision of what we hope to do, and we need supernatural power to enable the gospel to penetrate the hearts and minds of men and women, or all the doing in the world will be in vain.

2 Patrick Schreiner, *Acts*, Christian Standard Commentary (Holman Reference, 2021), 81.

3 Luke doesn't talk extensively about the kingdom of God in Acts, but the phrase occurs at important points at the beginning and end of the book (Acts 1:3, 6; 28:23, 31), as well as at important moments within the narrative (8:12; 14:22; 19:8; 20:25).

Put another way, what every church needs is momentum and not just movement. Movement can be aimless; momentum comes when everybody is moving in the same direction. Momentum by itself is not automatically good. Just ask a herd of lemmings. A church needs to be going in the *right* direction, led by the Holy Spirit. That is why, instead of going out and doing things, Jesus spends his precious last few days on earth instructing his disciples and pointing them to their need of power from on high, the gift of the Holy Spirit.

The Disciples' Need for Teaching

The need that the disciples still have for a great deal of instruction about the task that lies ahead of them can be seen from their question in Acts 1:6: "Lord, will you at this time restore the kingdom to Israel?"

Teachers may have told you early on in school that there is no such thing as a dumb question, but that is plainly false. Everyone who is an expert in anything knows that there are some questions that are just plain dumb or at least demonstrate a total lack of understanding of the field. No one who knows about sewing asks, "Which end of the needle am I supposed to use?" Similarly, no sports buff asks, "Why don't they run the football?" when it is fourth and twenty-seven with eight seconds on the clock. Those would be dumb questions—and this, too, is a dumb question. John Calvin comments that there are nearly as many errors in the disciples' question as there are words, which is quite an achievement.[4] The verb "restore" shows that they are still thinking in terms of a *political* kingdom, like the old kingdom of David. The noun "Israel" shows they are still thinking of a *national* kingdom made up of Abraham's descendants. Meanwhile, the phrase "at this time" suggests that they expect the coming of the kingdom to be an immediate, or at least an imminent, event. Jesus corrects each of these mistakes in verse 7; here we look at the content of Jesus's teaching in response to

4 John Calvin, *The Acts of the Apostles 1–13*, trans. John W. Fraser and W. J. G. McDonald, *Calvin's Commentaries*, ed. David W. Torrance and Thomas F. Torrance (Eerdmans; Paternoster, 1965), 29.

each of these mistakes in turn because it would be easy for us to fall into similar mistakes today.

What Jesus Teaches the Disciples

In his answer to the disciples' first mistake, Jesus points the disciples to the *spiritual* nature of the kingdom: "You will receive power when the Holy Spirit has come upon you, and you will be my witnesses" (Acts 1:8). God's kingdom is not a political kingdom that can be established by force or political intrigue, as most earthly kingdoms are. It will not come as the result of a coup or a democratic vote or a great marketing campaign. The church is not a business whose function is to maximize the number of its customers. On the contrary, it is a spiritual kingdom; its function is to bring together those worshipers whom God is calling to himself.

There are a number of ways in which we might fail to see the spiritual nature of the kingdom. On the one hand, we may be overly concerned about numbers. We may get excited when new people show up to church or discouraged if the turnout is low. But the numbers of people attending worship services may actually be a poor indicator of what God is doing by the power of his Spirit in the hearts and lives of individuals. Sometimes services with only a few people present may be of crucial significance in the life of an individual, while at other times there might be thousands present but no great work of the Spirit. Remember, we serve the shepherd who leaves the ninety-nine sheep on the hillside in search of the one lost sheep (Matt. 18:12–13). That's not necessarily good sheep management practice if your interest is maximizing the size of the flock. But it is the way God governs his kingdom: every single lost sheep matters to him and should likewise matter to us.

We might also spend too much time focusing on techniques to win people. There's certainly nothing wrong with studying how to present the gospel more clearly or thinking about what questions and presuppositions our society has that make it harder for people to hear the gospel. But in the end people are not converted by our understanding of apologetics or our mastery of the latest evangelistic strategy, helpful though those things may be. They are converted by the Holy Spirit. That should give us great boldness to speak even a simple word to our neighbor, trusting God to use it as he sees fit. It should also give us great motivation to pray for the Lord to set divine appointments in our day with people in whose lives he is already at work. I know that often I'm far too worried about whether I have the right argument to convince someone and not nearly confident enough in God's power to open closed ears and soften hard hearts. As a result, I say nothing, instead of speaking up and leaving the outcome to the Holy Spirit.

Another way to lose sight of the spiritual nature of the kingdom is to be overly obsessed by political process and influence. Certainly Christians should be responsible citizens and should vote wisely for the candidates who seem most likely to pursue justice and righteousness once elected. It is good that Christians should run for office and serve in various government positions, both locally and nationally. But our hope does not finally rest in who holds the power in Washington or Beijing or the Kremlin. Our hope rests in what Jesus is continuing to do from his exalted heavenly throne, from where he rules over the affairs of men and nations. He governs the decisions of unbelievers as well as believers: as Proverbs 21:1 reminds us, "The king's heart is a stream of water in the hand of the LORD; / he turns it wherever he will."

Jesus's kingdom will be established here on earth not through a moral majority taking back our culture but through men and women testifying about him in the power of the Holy Spirit. The Holy Spirit brings the church into existence and maintains her by empowering ordinary people to testify to Christ. In fact, this work of the Spirit is a major theme of the book of Acts: when the Holy Spirit comes, men and women receive power to witness, and the result is that a community of people who recognize Jesus as their King is established. That's ultimately always how real and lasting (positive) cultural change occurs: through the conversion of individuals who then live out their faith in all the different spheres of life, including politics. The primary mark of the presence of the Spirit of God in the book of Acts is not speaking in tongues or prophecy or signs and wonders but rather power to witness. When we pray in the Lord's Prayer for God's kingdom to come (Matt. 6:10), we are praying for him to pour out his Spirit on us so that we can be his witnesses and so that his church may be established and may grow.

Jesus also corrects the second mistake of his disciples by pointing to the *international* nature of God's kingdom: Jesus says, "You will be my witnesses in Jerusalem and in all Judea and Samaria, and to the end of the earth" (Acts 1:8). This verse is a miniature summary of the structure of the whole book of Acts: first of all, we see the apostles bearing witness in Jerusalem, then the message spreads to Judea and Samaria, then it heads to Antioch and the eastern Mediterranean, and finally the message comes to Rome itself, which was "the ends of the earth" from the perspective of Jerusalem.

The international character of the church may not seem like very surprising news to us in our modern era, but it was a revolutionary idea for the apostles. It was hard for them to grasp the fact that Jesus's kingdom would include not only Jews but also Gentiles and "half-breed" Samaritans. It has been said that in the Old Testament, we find concern for the nations but not the idea of a mission to the nations. Old Testament believers asserted that the nations would surely come to Israel's God (Isa. 2:2–4), but they would have been rather astonished by the idea that they should go to the nations and win them for Israel's God. Yet we have to ask, Is that attitude really so different from the actual practice of many churches and individual Christians today? We believe that God will save people from all over the world, perhaps, but do we expect this salvation to come by means of God bringing them to us here in church rather than by us going out to them and sharing the good news about Jesus? Perhaps you are hoping that God will do a mighty work in your church, but have you considered how that will happen except by you getting to know some of the people who live around you so that God can speak to them through you? Are you merely "concerned" that many people around you don't seem to know God, or do you see yourself as a missionary empowered by God's Spirit to bring the gospel to them?

What is more, how broad is your vision of the people God desires to reach? Sometimes we think the church's main task it is to make us comfortable and ensure that we are surrounded by the right kind of people—usually people just like us. On the contrary, Jesus constantly sends his disciples to those who are *not* like them, to pursue people who are not easy to like. After Jerusalem and Judea, they were to go to the hated Samaritans and then to the filthy Gentiles. Perhaps that was why there needed to be persecution in the early church, so that the early Christians would be forced to run for their lives and take the gospel out with them to new areas (Acts 8:1–4). Today, too, God sends us to the outcasts and the downtrodden, to the poor and the discriminated against, and to people who are going to make us feel uncomfortable. And he sends us both locally and to the ends of the earth. The healthy church does not have a unity that comes from everyone being alike, with common backgrounds and shared interests; it has a unity that comes from the gospel and the common salvation that we share in Christ. Indeed, a healthy church has a unity that is humanly inexplicable, given the diversity of backgrounds that are represented, yet a unity that comes naturally when a body of people are welded together by the power of the Spirit.

When Will the Kingdom Be Restored?

Although the disciples ask, "Lord, will *you* at this time restore the kingdom to Israel?" (Acts 1:6), Jesus replies, "You will receive power when the Holy Spirit has come upon you, and *you* will be my witnesses" (1:8). That's an interesting shift. It provides a counterweight for the point we made earlier about learning before doing. Learning about God and the Bible is never a substitute for doing; it is a necessary equipping for the sake of obedient and effective doing. In your prayers, are you merely praying for God to do the work while hoping that he would send others to accomplish that work, or are you praying for God to empower *you* to do his work as he provides opportunity?

It is in this context that Jesus rebukes the disciples' concern with the timescale of God's plans: "It is not for you to know the times or periods that the Father has set by his own authority" (1:7). Jesus means that a keen interest in the times and dates of his return can easily become a distraction for Christians, even an excuse for not doing the work we have been given to do. As Deuteronomy 29:29 puts it, "The secret things belong to the LORD our God, but the things that are revealed belong to us and to our children forever, that we may do all the words of this law." There are some things that God is not going to tell us, including the date of Christ's return. Meanwhile, there are plenty of things that he has made known to us—in fact, everything we need for our life and growth in godliness and for presenting the gospel to our neighbors. It is more profitable for us to put our energies into studying and obeying those things than it is for us to get caught up in trying to work out exactly when Jesus is coming back.

Of course, there are dangers on both sides, whether you think that the date of Jesus's return will be soon or a long time away. In both cases it is possible to forget the task at hand. For instance, if you think that Jesus is going to return next week, you won't have much interest in reaching the whole world for Christ. You'll have no time to prepare any long-term plans or to take any interest in pursuing the *shalom* of wherever God has placed you (Jer. 29:7). But equally, if you think that Jesus's return is a far-off event, you may not sense any urgency to pursue his kingdom in the meantime.

Jesus makes that clear in the parable of the talents in Matthew 25. In the parable, a man goes away and entrusts his servants with different amounts of money. The first servant is faithful with his ten talents, the second is faithful with his five, but the third goes away and hides his one talent (Matt. 25:15–18). When the master comes back, he rebukes his servant (25:26–27): Why didn't he at least take his one talent to the bank where it would have earned interest? Many sermons on this passage make the point that we're all supposed to be faithful with what God has given us and not mind that he has given other people more. That is certainly true, but there is more to the parable.

The whole parable is based on the premise that the master will be away a considerable time. After all, a week's interest on a small sum of money would hardly be worth getting worked up about. Did the unfaithful servant expect his master back very soon—in which case, it was hardly worth bothering to be busy for him in the meantime? Or did he expect that he would never come back—in which case he would never have to account for his laziness? Either way, the difference between the faithful and the unfaithful servants is that the master finds the faithful servants busily doing their duty when he returns. It is the same way with the return of the Lord Jesus: never mind when it is going to happen; make sure that you are busy doing what he has commissioned you to do in the present.

That is why the disciples receive a rebuke from two angels after Christ's ascension. There the disciples stand, looking up into the sky. The angels say to them, "Why do you stand looking into heaven? This Jesus, who was taken up from you into heaven, will come in the same way as you saw him go into heaven" (Acts 1:11). In one sense, it is only natural that the disciples should be straining their eyes for a last earthly glimpse of Jesus. But in another sense, their gaze is fixed in entirely the wrong direction. As John Stott puts it, "There was something fundamentally anomalous with their gazing up into the sky when they had been commissioned to go to the ends of the earth."[5]

The ascension marks an important transition: It is the end of the earthly ministry of Jesus and the beginning of the heavenly ministry of Jesus. Jesus is now at the right hand of the Father as anticipated in Daniel 7:13–14. He is interceding for us daily, and he is building his kingdom. At the same time, the ascension marks the beginning of the time between the times, the time between Jesus's first and second coming, the time for the church to begin her task of mission to the ends of the earth in the power of the Holy Spirit, whom the ascended Jesus is about to pour out.

This is the time in which we too find ourselves. Now is not the time for a nostalgic looking up into heaven, waiting for Jesus, but for

5 John R. W. Stott, *The Message of Acts: To the Ends of the Earth*, The Bible Speaks Today (InterVarsity Press, 1990), 51.

a visionary and compassionate looking out to a lost and dying world. You don't need constantly to be standing and staring up into the sky because when Jesus comes back, you won't miss him! His coming will be glorious and unmistakable, an event universally seen and recognized. Even more than that, you shouldn't just be standing there looking up because Jesus has given you a task to do here on earth: take the good news to all creation (Mark 16:15).

A fundamental dynamic is thus at work in the closing part of this passage. Jesus Christ has gone up into heaven; as a result, the Spirit will be sent down from there by the ascended Jesus, enabling you to go out in his power, and then, when that earthly ingathering is complete, Christ will come back. In that dynamic, we also live where the bulk of the book of Acts lives: between the coming of the Spirit and the second coming of Jesus. Therefore, we too are called to share in the task of taking the gospel to all nations in the power of the Holy Spirit (Matt. 28:19–20).

What Are You Waiting For?

As we await Christ's return, what does Jesus need to teach you today? Perhaps you need to wait while you are instructed more adequately in biblical truth—or on the other hand, you might need to get out in the power of the Spirit and witness to the things you already know. Maybe you view the church as a business that exists to maximize its consumers or as a country club that exists to satisfy the needs and desires of its members. Have you been more concerned with debating the fine points of theology or the date of the end times than you have with your mission as a witness to the world? We all have much to repent of.

This passage, however, also offers great encouragement. Those eleven men whose only question to Jesus in this passage is a dumb one were the same men who, when the Spirit was poured out, turned the world upside down (Acts 17:6). The transformation did not come from them attending a seminar on witnessing techniques; it lay instead in the pouring out of God's Spirit. The reality is that the Spirit uses dumb and incompetent people *like us* to achieve his sublime purposes of saving his chosen people. Of course, that's not really a surprise if you understand the gospel truth that the only thing we bring to our salvation is our sin. We come to Jesus as spiritually blind men and women needing to see. We come as spiritually weary people needing rest. We come as spiritually dead people needing new life. All this God does for us in Christ through the Holy Spirit. He takes us just as we are and shapes us slowly and painstakingly into showcases of his grace. Out of these showcases of his grace, broken and damaged though we are, God builds his church. Our weakness is the context for his strength to be radically demonstrated.

Jesus says, "You will be my witnesses in Jerusalem and in all Judea and Samaria, and to the end of the earth" (1:8). This international commission is a big challenge. Our mission is to win the world for Jesus Christ. If it were presented to us in the terms of the old *Mission Impossible* franchise ("Your mission, should you choose to accept it . . ."), most of us would probably decline: "Here am I, Lord; please send someone else." The task overwhelms us—as indeed it should. How could *I* possibly change a cold, dead heart of stone into a heart of living flesh? We need to remember that Jesus didn't leave us alone to do the job. He has done the job himself. Jesus first came down from the comforts of heaven to earth and surrounded himself with people who were hard to love. He didn't get sidetracked from his mission or back down from it in the way we so often do. Instead, Jesus went out empowered by the gospel to preach good news to Jews and Gentiles, gathering broken reeds that in his gentleness he would not break. Out of these broken and shattered people, he built his church, and he promises to continue to build his church through us. The church of Christ is founded on the solid rock of his death, resurrection, and ascension. The gates of hell cannot and will not prevail against it (Matt. 16:18).

Jesus promises us his presence and his power to continue to accomplish his purposes through us. He is still at work in and through the church, accomplishing all his holy will. As he told the disciples right before he left them, "I am with you always, to the end of the age" (Matt. 28:20), and, "You will receive power when the Holy Spirit has come upon you" (Acts 1:8). His presence and his power are what turns the impossible mission of reaching the world for Jesus Christ not only into "mission possible" but into a certain accomplishment. Luke writes, "In the first book, O Theophilus, I have dealt with all that Jesus began to do and teach" (Acts 1:1). But the earth itself could not contain the books that tell the story of what Jesus has continued to do through the power of his Spirit in ordinary Christians ever since then. Broken vessels, indwelled by the Spirit, are the tools that Jesus uses in bringing many broken people from all kinds of backgrounds to become worshipers of our great and mighty God so that they might be showcases of his grace and mercy.

2

Waiting for God

Acts 1:12–26

ELTON JOHN WAS WRONG. Actually, Sir Elton (to give him his full title) has been wrong about many things, but in particular, I think that he was wrong when he sang that "sorry seems to be the hardest word."[1] Yes, it is sometimes hard to genuinely apologize for doing something wrong, but if Sir Elton had spent more time around children, perhaps he would know that "sorry" is sometimes pretty easy to say, especially if you don't have to sound as if you mean it. In reality, sorry is not always the hardest word. A much harder word, especially for children but also for the rest of us, is "wait." Wait until your birthday; then you can open your present. Wait until your paycheck comes before you buy that new couch. Wait for exams to be over and summer to begin. In my experience, the word "wait" is a whole lot harder than "sorry."

"Wait" is what Jesus told the disciples to do before he left them and ascended into heaven: "And while staying with them he ordered them not to depart from Jerusalem, but to wait for the promise of the Father" (Acts 1:4). That is exactly what they do. In this passage, we see what the disciples spend their time doing while they wait. They don't spend

1 "Sorry Seems to Be the Hardest Word," by Elton John and Bernie Taupin, recorded March 22, 1976, MCA Records.

their time doing crosswords or playing video games; they don't fill up their days watching television or following the sporting exploits of the Jerusalem Jaguars. Instead, we see them doing two things that are models for us to copy: praying in faith and preparing in faith.

Praying in Faith

To begin with, we are told that the eleven apostles meet together with the women, and with Mary the mother of Jesus and his brothers, joining constantly in prayer (Acts 1:12–14). Luke highly values women in a way that wasn't common in the ancient world, and so they appear regularly in his account of the early church. It is Luke who tells us the story of Martha and Mary, with Martha distractedly busy in the kitchen while Mary sits at Jesus's feet, choosing the "good portion" (Luke 10:38–42). Here, Luke notes that even though none of the apostles are women, the women aren't simply shoved aside to join Martha in the kitchen; they too join in the important task of prayer with the apostles.

There are two specific aspects to the prayers of the early Christians that Luke wants us to see. The first aspect is the consistency and persistency of their prayer: they are constantly found praying together (Acts 1:14). The early believers didn't just meet together once in a while for a prayer meeting. They didn't just open and close their meetings in prayer. Rather, they were devoted to prayer. This is a serious challenge to me personally because I don't think that the same could be said of me. Instead, I'm constantly and persistently busy. Like Martha, I'm devoted to doing many good things, but I'm not nearly so constantly and persistently engaged in prayer, either individually or together with other believers. I'm convicted by this attitude of the first apostles and challenged to reorder my priorities, as perhaps you are. Prayer is really difficult for most of us, and few of our churches seem to be constantly and persistently devoted to prayer.

In order for that to change, we need to reorder our thinking about the church, to make our practice fit with our theory. When we commit ourselves to pray, we are reminding ourselves that what is really important is what God does in this world, not what we do. What will make or break our church as an effective part of God's spiritual kingdom is not the number of small group meetings that we organize or the evangelistic campaigns that we run or the good deeds we do in our community. It is not even the number of great sermons that we hear. The greatest sermons in the world will have no impact unless the Holy Spirit opens the hearts of those who listen, including us. The greatest evangelization campaign has no power to convert people apart from the intervention of the Holy Spirit to bring new life into the hearts and minds of spiritually dead men and women. The best-run programs to help men, women, youth, or families will be of little value if they are simply an expression of our own efforts. But when God takes up our rather feeble efforts, he will accomplish whatever he desires. If God is at work in our hearts and, through us, in our community, then people will be changed and God will be glorified in and through our churches.

We believe that in theory, of course, but that belief is not always evident from the way we operate. We may say that we are desperately needy people who can do nothing without Christ, but then we often persist in acting as if we were perfectly competent by ourselves to accomplish anything we set our minds to. Even when we feel overwhelmed by life's circumstances, very often prayer is quite literally the last thing that we think to do. Yet if we really believed that only God can accomplish his holy purposes for us and for our church, that conviction would commit us to far more persistent and constant prayer.

What is more, prayer is not merely a more effective way of getting through our to-do lists. Prayer brings us into the presence of our heavenly Father, who loves us and cares deeply for us. When we fail to pray, we are acting like the spiritual orphans that we very often think ourselves to be, deep down in our hearts. But if we have a loving Father who delights to walk with us through life, to delight in our moments of triumph and to surround us with his arms in our moments of pain and despair, why wouldn't we run to talk to him all the time?

Praying Together

The other aspect of their prayer that Luke highlights here is the fact that the disciples pray "with one accord" (Acts 1:14). This means more than simply the fact that they are all praying in the same place at the same time. They are united; they are of one mind in their prayers. They do not merely pray as individuals for their own individual needs and desires; rather, they put their minds together as well as their voices to pray for their common needs and aspirations. They bear one another's burdens together before the throne of grace (Gal. 6:2). This too is something we can imitate. Such a bearing of burdens can happen in many different contexts: when individuals meet together spontaneously for prayer, as part of a women's Bible study or a men's meeting, or when the whole church assembles every week to pray. We have the privilege, as individuals and as a church, to meet together and to link our hearts together regularly in prayer.

We are intensely affected by the individualism of our culture—perhaps especially those of us who are men. Men are encouraged by our society to model ourselves on the image of the rugged outdoorsman, driving our own 4x4 pickup truck across a solitary landscape, making our own decisions, running our own life without reference to anyone else. Sometimes that pattern was reinforced through our interactions with our own fathers. But we are called to be an interdependent body of believers, not an assortment of free-floating toenails and eyelashes (1 Cor. 12:18–26), and one of the ways we can express our membership in Christ's body is by meeting to pray together in one accord. You don't need permission from the pastor or elders to do this: find someone else within the church and plan to meet regularly for prayer so that you constantly remind one another that it is God whose work is really significant in the church.

Preparing for Mission

Praying isn't the only thing that the disciples do while they wait, however. They also prepare in faith for the task ahead—by finding another apostle to take Judas's place. And once again there are lessons for us to learn.

In the first place, we need to learn a godly fear from the fate of Judas. The name *Judas* has for us become so intertwined with the concept of betrayal that it is hard for us to put ourselves in the shoes of the first apostles and experience their shock at his demise. In the space of a few days, Judas goes from being a trusted member of the inner circle, an apostle, one with whom they had eaten and journeyed for three solid years, to a traitor who sells their Lord for thirty pieces of silver and then dies by his own hand (Matt. 27:3–8; Acts 1:16–19). Just how shocking this series of events is to the disciples can be seen from their reaction when Jesus tells them at the Last Supper that one of them will betray him (Matt. 26:21). They don't turn to one another and say, "Well, we all know who that will be. I never liked that Judas guy. He's a shifty character if ever there was one." No, their response is for each of them to say, "Is it I?" (Matt. 26:22). It is more believable to them that they themselves should betray Jesus than that one of the other apostles would do it, so high is their confidence and trust in one another. But nonetheless, Judas betrays his Lord.

If Judas can betray Jesus, why not someone else? It would have been natural for the loss of Judas to have struck fear into each of their hearts. There is a certain appropriateness to that fear as well. "Why not me? Why wouldn't I betray the Lord too? I'm not more noble of heart than Judas, and I certainly haven't been better taught and discipled than Judas was. He spent three years being schooled twenty-four hours a day by Jesus himself! So how can I be confident that I will remain faithful to the end?" The answer is that as long as my confidence is in myself, I had better be very afraid. No matter what degrees I hold, what positions in the church I have occupied, what ministries I have engaged in, none of that will keep me faithful to the Lord. Judas is merely the first in a long line of men who were once leaders in the church and then made a shipwreck of their faith (1 Tim. 1:19). Left to myself, I could just as easily abandon my faith and betray my Lord as Judas did. If considering the fate of Judas makes me less confident in myself, that is certainly a good kind of fear to have.

But the focus of the passage is not on reasons for fear but on reasons for confidence. One apostle may have deserted the faith, but the other eleven are still here: just read the list of names in Acts 1:13. The eleven who run away and abandon Jesus at his arrest are all restored to their place of ministry. Not only are they present but so too are Jesus's mother and his brothers (1:14). Remember, Jesus's brothers are earlier among the skeptics. In John 7:5, we read that "not even his brothers believed in him." But now they do. The work of grace has been extended to those who formerly doubted so that they have been brought to faith. This is an important counter-reality to the reality of Judas's abandoning the faith. The gospel that will go to the ends of the earth by the end of the book of Acts first bears fruit closer to home in Jesus's immediate family, bringing hard-hearted skeptics to belief.

Judas's abandoning of the faith and betrayal of the Lord is itself a fulfillment of the Scriptures (Acts 1:16). This act of wickedness and sin is not a rogue element in the world, something operating outside God's sovereignty and control. On the contrary, even this terrible crime is prophesied by the Holy Spirit in the book of Psalms (Acts 1:20; cf. Ps. 69:25; 109:8). That is surely a remarkable fact. What act could be more wickedly sinful than to betray the Messiah and hand him over to his death? This is rebellion against the living God at its most foul and blatant. Yet the wickedness of man in its highest, grossest form can do nothing other than what God has previously determined in his holy will. God is absolutely sovereign over even the very worst sin.

What is more, Peter tells us that the Scriptures also anticipated another man being raised up to take Judas's place (Acts 1:20). It could never permanently be Jesus and the eleven apostles. That would suggest that Jesus's mission has been partially unsuccessful, incomplete at least in this one point. He hasn't been able to preserve twelve apostles.

Never! There could no more be eleven apostles than there could be eleven tribes of Israel. The number twelve was God's plan from the beginning, and it will continue to be the plan. Another apostle will have to be raised up to take up the ministry that Judas abandoned, just as God had promised.

Finding a New Apostle

Filling that place is not simply a matter of finding a volunteer or electing the most popular person. The ministry of apostleship, like all positions of leadership in Christ's church, required someone who was qualified for the task. The qualifications of apostleship are simple and straightforward: an apostle had to have been part of Jesus's three-year training program, from its beginnings in the ministry of John the Baptist to its end with his ascension (Acts 1:22). An apostle was an eyewitness of Jesus's ministry, and especially of Jesus's resurrection, so he had to have been there all along in order to testify to what he had heard and seen and handled and touched (1 John 1:1–3). That's one reason why we cannot have apostles in the church anymore. There are no more people who fit these qualifications, so the office of apostle has necessarily ceased. Indeed, the pool of candidates is quite a restricted group in the early chapters of Acts—so restricted that there are only two suitable candidates: Joseph Barsabbas and Matthias (Acts 1:23).

There's one other qualification for the replacement apostle that we could easily miss. In verse 21, Peter specifies that the replacement apostle must be "one of the men" who accompanied Jesus throughout his ministry. This is a necessary distinction since there were, of course, also women who journeyed with Jesus (Luke 23:49). Both men and women can equally be disciples of Jesus, and both have important roles to play in the church. But the authoritative leadership and teaching function associated with the apostles is restricted to men, just as is the pattern elsewhere in the Bible.

At this point in Acts, the early church has to choose between these two candidates. They both can't be apostles, or there will be thirteen apostles, not twelve. Nor can the early church add to God's list of qualifications, any more than they can take from it. Both men are qualified to be apostles, and so the only question is which one is called to the task. Their answer once again shows the early disciples' dependence on God every step of the way. First, they pray over the decision (1:24). They ask God, the searcher of hearts, to choose between these two equally qualified candidates. Then they draw lots between them, putting the decision in God's own hands—for "the lot is cast into the lap, / but its every decision is from the LORD" (Prov. 16:33). An apostle is not appointed by men but by God, and casting lots is the disciples' way of making that fact abundantly clear. Since Jesus has chosen the other apostles during his earthly ministry, it is important that the risen Jesus also choose the replacement apostle.

Is this decision-making method also a model for us so that we too should draw lots in order to seek guidance from God? Sometimes Christians are tempted to approach their circumstances as material for divination, as the pagans did, often using Gideon's fleece in the book of Judges as biblical justification (Judg. 6:36–40). When Gideon wanted confirmation that God really would be with him when he went out to battle against the Midianites, he asked God that a fleece he had laid out overnight would be wet with dew but the ground around it dry (6:36–37).When God answered his request in the affirmative, Gideon asked for further confirmation. On the next night he said to God, "Let it be dry on the fleece only, and on all the ground let there be dew" (6:38–39).

This is not a Christian approach to decision-making, however. Indeed, Gideon is not presented as a model for us in his practice at this point. Gideon's fleeces are rather a sign of his lack of faith in the Lord than a positive example: the angel of the Lord has personally appeared to him to call him as Israel's judge (Judg. 6:11–27), the Spirit of the Lord has empowered Gideon and raised an army for him (6:34–35), and Gideon himself acknowledges that the Lord has told him that he will save Israel by Gideon's hand. Yet he still needs a sign if he is going to believe God's word! And when the Lord gives him the first sign (the fleece wet and the surrounding ground dry), he promptly requests a second sign with the ground wet and the fleece dry.

In fact, if you read on in Gideon's story, you discover that he isn't even convinced by the two fleeces: he isn't confident of the Lord's presence with him until he goes down to the Midianites' camp and overhears one Midianite telling another about a bizarre dream he's had about a loaf of barley bread destroying the camp, which he interprets as evidence that the Israelites are certain to win (7:10–15). Gideon's fleece is actually a sign of just how bad things are in Israel in Gideon's days, not a guide for how modern Christians should make important life choices.

It is striking to notice, therefore, that whereas the apostolic number is completed by drawing lots, the early church doesn't draw lots to choose the first deacons in Acts 6, or to discern who should be elders in 1 Timothy 3. There is something unique about this circumstance in Acts 1 that calls for casting lots. After all, the Spirit of the Lord has not yet been poured out on the church: that doesn't happen until the day of Pentecost in Acts 2.

Now that the gift of the Spirit has been given to the church, the normal decision-making process for believers in our period of redemptive history is by means of prayer and the wise evaluation of the different alternatives in counsel with other mature believers. That's not to say that God doesn't ever guide us through our circumstances. Sometimes you have two choices in front of you, both of which are good, and there seems to be nothing to choose between them. It wouldn't be wrong to say, "I'll go with whichever one responds first." Providence can sometimes confirm and encourage us in a particular direction. The point, however, is that our reading of providence is always flawed and fallible and should not be the ultimate basis for our decision-making. It must always be tested through the primary grids of Scripture and wise counsel.

The main point of the passage, though, is not the method that the apostles choose to seek God's leading. The main point is that the Lord answers their prayers, gives his people the guidance they seek, and shows clearly his will for them in appointing Matthias as a replacement apostle to take Judas's place (Acts 1:26). The number of the twelve is once again complete. When the Holy Spirit comes, they will be ready to begin the task appointed for them by the Lord Jesus of bringing the gospel to the ends of the earth.

The Lord Keeps His Own

This brings us back to the striking contrast that lies at the heart of this passage. On the one hand, you have Judas, a man whose life is so full of promise but ends up in the shame and waste of suicide and under the judgment of God. On the other, you have Peter, a man who denies his Lord three times (Luke 22:61) and yet is nonetheless restored to leadership by Jesus (see John 20), a man who here stands up boldly as the spokesman of the new community. Alongside Peter, we see eleven other men who are nobodies, humanly speaking, but who with God's empowering are about to turn the world upside down (see Acts 17:6).

What makes the difference between Judas and Peter and the other apostles? It is not that the other apostles are more gifted or more faithful or more worthy than Judas. It is only the grace of God and the protecting power of the Lord Jesus that preserves his apostles from ruin. Jesus himself says as much in his high priestly prayer in John 17:12: "While I was with them, I kept them in your name, which you have given me. I have guarded them, and not one of them has been lost except the son of destruction, that the Scripture might be fulfilled." The Lord's protection makes the difference. Nor is that protection going to be withdrawn from them now that Jesus has returned to heaven. By the power of the Holy Spirit, God continues to protect his apostles. God's grace and protecting power are similarly extended today to all those who are genuinely his people.

There is both good news and bad news here for us. First the bad news: Jesus's definition of protection doesn't always match ours. Jesus's protection of his apostles doesn't exclude them being beheaded as happens to James, or stoned to death as apparently happens to Matthias, or being crucified upside down as happens to Peter. The Lord's protection is never protection from adverse circumstances but rather protection *through* adverse circumstances. It is the Lord's protection that enables us to remain faithful in our devotion to him amid the worst that this world can throw at us. There is no surprise here. After all, Jesus himself says that no disciple is ever greater than his master: "If they persecuted me, they will also persecute you" (John 15:20). The Christian life is often hard, but God is always faithful to keep all those who are his. No one and nothing in all creation can snatch you out of his hand, if you belong to him (10:28). That is good news indeed!

Yet there is even better news in this passage for all those who ever feel like Judas. We have all let down the Lord and betrayed him in thought, word, and deed. In fact, we all act like Judas each and every time we sin. Whenever we sin, we are following Judas in betraying our Lord. Like him, we put something else in first place in our lives ahead of our commitment to God. We may not sell our Lord for thirty pieces of silver; indeed, we often sell him for far less—the momentary satisfaction of our desires. If, as I sometimes do, you feed your pride and sense of self-importance by making cutting remarks about someone else—attacking their appearance or their performance or their lack of relational skills—you have betrayed the Lord by degrading a person made in his image. If you use food or shopping or internet pornography to medicate away your worries, you have run to a refuge apart from God. At that moment, you are saying that this feeling of power, pleasure, control, or pretended intimacy is more important to you than your commitment to the Lord Jesus. The reality is that we are all repeat offenders at betraying Jesus.

The good news for Judases like us lies in the work of the Holy Spirit, who brings us to repentance. The difference between us and Judas is not his sin—we are exactly like him in that. The difference is in our repentance, which is a work of God in our hearts, delivering us from eternal death. It is God who, by his grace, makes us hate our sin and long for deliverance from it (Rom. 7:21–25). God protects those whom he has called his own so that we are not utterly undone and destroyed by our sin but instead learn to repent of it and to run to the cross with it, there to find the mercy and grace we need. That is what Judas was not able to do, and as a result his sin destroyed him. That is what God in his mercy and grace enables us to do so that, far from destroying us, even our worst sin leads us into a deeper love for God and a more profound appreciation of the vastness of his grace to us in the gospel. If God was able to preserve his first fickle and wandering apostles, he can surely preserve us.

Jesus, the Ultimate Apostle

God is able to show us this grace of forgiveness because Jesus was no Judas: he was the true "apostle"—for the Greek word translated "apostle" simply means someone who has been sent as a delegate, envoy, or messenger.[2] Jesus was sent by the Father and never betrayed his calling to redeem his people from their sins. In the wilderness, Jesus repeatedly refuses to compromise his commitment to God's word when he is put to the test by Satan (Matt. 4:1–11). He never took the easy path of sin that we so often choose. Jesus did not betray his calling in the garden of Gethsemane either. When he was under enormous spiritual and psychological pressure, he said, "Not my will, but yours, be done" (Luke 22:42). Jesus took that stance of perpetual faithfulness all the way to the cursed death of the cross so that rebellious and treasonous sinners like us might be spared that fate. Jesus's perfect obedience to the Father's calling stands in place of our continual rebellion against him and becomes the means by which we are enabled to enter the Father's life-giving presence.

If you are not yet a believer in Christ, Judas's fate issues you with a stark challenge. How are you any different from him? You too have rebelled in thought, word, and deed against the God who created you. When you stand before that same God on the last day, what will be your defense? There is only one defense that endures, which is the perfect righteousness of Christ, received as a free gift through faith (Eph. 2:8–10).

But if you have put your trust in Jesus Christ, you need have no fear about your fate, no matter how weak and how full of sin you know yourself to be. Those whom God has chosen and called he will justify. He declares us righteous for the sake of Christ's righteousness in which we stand. Those whom he calls he will also sanctify, transforming us slowly into the image of his Son. Ultimately, all those whom the Father calls he will also glorify in his Son, giving us the wonderful inheritance that he has prepared for all his people (Rom. 8:28–30). Only in Christ can you ever hope to persevere against all the assaults of Satan. He alone can keep you faithfully trusting him until he comes back—and he certainly will keep you faithful if you belong to him. Those whom Jesus holds firmly in his hands will never be snatched away from his loving grasp. We belong to him, and we will be his forever.

2 Frederick W. Danker, Walter Bauer, William D. Arndt, and F. Wilbur Gingrich, *A Greek-English Lexicon of the New Testament and Other Early Christian Literature*, 3rd ed. (University of Chicago Press, 2000), 122.

3

Power from on High

Acts 2:1–21

SOMETIMES THE EVENTS of a single day change your life forever. The day I got married was one of those days for me. I woke up single. I spent the day in a frenzy of joyful—and sometimes harried—busyness. Then, when it was all over, my situation in life was entirely different from what it was only a few hours earlier. Now I was married. My wedding was a life-changing event that I will remember for the rest of my life.

The day of Pentecost is just such a day in the life of the church. This is the day when the church receives the gift that Jesus has promised her: the Holy Spirit comes upon the disciples and imparts to them power to witness—the power to carry out their appointed task of sharing with the entire world the good news about Jesus Christ. After Pentecost, the church is never the same.

Pentecost and the Giving of the Law

The festival of Pentecost is a particularly appropriate day for the Spirit to be poured out on God's people, bringing about this great transformation in the life of the church. We may miss the significance of the fact that the pouring out of the Spirit happens at Pentecost because for us as Christians, Pentecost has become identified with the events recounted here in the book of Acts. But Pentecost was originally a

Jewish festival—better known to Bible readers as the Feast of Weeks because it came seven weeks after the Passover. The connection of the events of this day with what preceded them in the Old Testament is highlighted by Luke speaking of the time "when the day of Pentecost arrived" (Acts 2:1). By the time of Jesus, Pentecost had become the festival at which the Jews celebrated the giving of the law on Mount Sinai. In fact, what we see in the beginning of Acts 2 looks very much like a miniature version of the events on Mount Sinai: we hear of a violent wind, of fire, and of voices, all of which were elements of God's self-revelation on the mountain (Ex. 19). But all this symbolism is now associated not with the giving of the law but with the pouring out of God's Holy Spirit.

That is a very significant change. The trouble with the giving of the law in the time of Moses was that it only brought about a change in the external state of the people. Outwardly they entered a covenant relationship with the Lord, but inwardly their hearts remained unchanged. In that respect, the giving of the law was a lot like getting married: legally, once you are married, you are in an entirely different relationship to your spouse, but on the inside you are still the same person you were when you woke up that morning. That reality comes as a great shock to many who hoped that getting married would somehow magically transform them or their spouses into better people. Getting married doesn't change a person's heart, however; it changes only his or her external state. Of course, over time, marriage changes both parties profoundly, for better or worse—but this change doesn't happen immediately!

So, too, when Moses came down from the mountain to give God's people the good news of God's law, he discovered they had broken several of the Ten Commandments before they had even received them (see Ex. 32:1–6). That was a remarkable achievement. They were bowing down to the golden calf before the ink on "You shall not make for yourself a carved image" was even dry! What is more, this was no temporary aberration. It is the story of Israel's history: the people started as they meant to go on, breaking God's law again and again. Before we get too judgmental toward Israel, however, isn't lawbreaking the story of your life and mine? I don't know about you, but I'm routinely convicted by the Scriptures about areas of my life that do not conform to God's law. My actions and my words—never mind my thoughts—don't come close to measuring up to God's perfect standard. I don't love the Lord with all my heart, mind, soul, and strength, nor do I love my neighbor as myself (Matt. 22:36–40). Indeed, even in those rare moments when I actually do the things I ought to do, I know that my motives for doing so are often entirely self-centered. I obey God so that people will think I am a wonderful person or because I'm afraid of the shame that would come from being caught breaking God's law—not because I genuinely want to serve and glorify him. I am no better than the ancient Israelites.

You might wonder, then, why anyone with half a brain would want a festival to celebrate the giving of the law. Why would we celebrate something that continually condemns us? That seems like turkeys celebrating Thanksgiving or armadillos celebrating interstate highways. Yet the Old Testament itself recognized that there would be more to the law than simply an opportunity to wallow in guilt. Once the law had done its work of pointing out the impossibility of pleasing God in our own strength, a new era of obedience would be given. This is what the Lord has to say through the prophet Ezekiel:

> I will take you from the nations and gather you from all the countries and bring you into your own land. I will sprinkle clean water on you, and you shall be clean from all your uncleannesses, and from all your idols I will cleanse you. And I will give you a new heart, and a new spirit I will put within you. And I will remove the heart of stone from your flesh and give you a heart of flesh. And I will put my Spirit within you, and cause you to walk in my statutes and be careful to obey my rules. You shall dwell in the land that I gave to your fathers, and you shall be my people, and I will be your God. (Ezek. 36:24–28; cf. Deut. 30:6)

The Lord promised a new era in the last days in which the Lord's Spirit would be poured out on his people and they would lead purified lives with the law written on their hearts. That expectation finds its initial fulfillment at Pentecost: the noise like a violent wind symbolizes power, and the tongues of fire symbolize purity. Both are poured out on the church through the Spirit (Acts 2:2–3).

Christians, who live in the era when the Spirit has been poured out, have a new level of power to live holy lives that please God. That doesn't mean that we now live under the law, seeking to win approval from God by our obedience. The law still always condemns us because, even as Spirit-filled Christians, we always fall very far short of its perfect standard. As the Heidelberg Catechism reminds us, in this life even the best people make only small beginnings on the pathway to holiness.[1] To adopt the language of the old Puritan prayer "The Valley of Vision," "I live in the depths but see thee in the heights; hemmed in by mountains of sin I behold thy glory."[2] If you are a Christian, Jesus Christ has won God's complete approval for you by what he has done in your place, not by your own best efforts. As the apostle Paul says, "I have been crucified with Christ" (Gal. 2:20). On the cross, not only was Jesus executed but, in a sense, we, too, were executed—all of us who have placed our trust in him for our salvation. This means that on the cross the just penalty for every one of our sins—past, present and future—was paid in full, so the law has no further claims on us. If you are a believer in Christ, your failures to keep the law are done away with, and the condemnation you rightly deserve for your continual self-centeredness and self-glorification is completely paid for.

More than that, Christ not only paid the penalty the law demanded from us but fulfilled the perfect obedience that the law requires. Christ did not set the law aside, as if it were a bad thing that got in the way of you living life to the full. No, the law is good and holy, an expression of God's perfect will (Rom. 7:12). That is why Jesus had to come and live his life here on earth, not merely be beamed down

1 Question 114 of The Heidelberg Catechism, in *Creeds, Confessions and Catechisms: A Reader's Edition*, ed. Chad Van Dixhoorn (Crossway, 2022), 327.

2 Arthur Bennett, ed., "The Valley of Vision," in *The Valley of Vision: A Collection of Puritan Prayers and Devotions* (Banner of Truth, 1988), xv.

onto the cross. He had to be born under the law and fulfill it (Matt. 5:17), living a perfect life for us by fulfilling the law's just and holy demands in our place.

Not only has Christ fulfilled the law *for* us; he is now continuing to fulfill the law *through* us. It is not only true that "I have been crucified with Christ" but also that "I no longer live, but Christ lives in me" (Gal. 2:20). Christ continues to fulfill the law through us by his Holy Spirit, poured out on his church at Pentecost. Remember the introduction to the book of Acts. Luke said, "In the first book, O Theophilus, I have dealt with all that Jesus began to do and teach" (Acts 1:1). Now in this second book—the one we now call "Acts"—we see what Jesus continues to do and teach through his church by his Spirit. So, then, the coming of the Holy Spirit is the fulfillment of the festival of Pentecost as a celebration of the giving of the law: the power has been poured out on his people to begin the process of changing them into those who love and obey God's perfect law, as we will see at the end of Acts 2.

The Spirit, the Christian, and the Law

There are, I think, two very practical implications of Pentecost. First, it means that no Christian is beyond hope. At the end of the Old Testament, a faithful believer might have been tempted to give up on Israel. The people of Israel had so many advantages—they had God's promises to Abraham, the miraculous deliverance out of Egypt, God's perfect and holy law, and his word delivered through the prophets. Yet time after time, they had failed God and broken his covenant, and they experienced the curses of Sinai as a result. When would they ever learn? Even the people who returned from exile in Babylon struggled with many of the same sins as their forefathers (see Ezra and Nehemiah). Yet the promise of a new covenant revealed in Jeremiah 31:31–34 reminded Israel that the Lord had not given up on them. He would one day pour out his Spirit on them (see Ezek. 36:24–28 above) and bring about their full salvation. Pentecost showed that God still had good plans for his people, in spite of themselves, and he would bring those plans to fruition.

In the same way, it is tempting for us to write off some people as hopeless, thinking that they will never change. Perhaps a family member or a friend is a believer in the Lord but has charted a course away from the Lord or is struggling with a besetting sin that seems impossible to shake. You yourself may even be tempted to give up on Christ, given the depth of your own indwelling sin. "How can I be a Christian and still be in bondage to this pattern of sin after so many years?," you might say. "I guess it's just who I am." In Western culture, we sometimes feed this perspective by placing labels on people: you are a bulimic; you are a homosexual; or you are a person with an obsessive-compulsive disorder. No! If you are a Christian, these labels are *not* who you are. They may indeed describe who you once were or map out the contours of your present struggle for sanctification. But they are not your identity. You *are* a Christian, a saint, and the Holy Spirit is doing an irresistible work inside you, so it must reach a successful conclusion.

Pentecost thus means that we can never give up on people, because if someone is a Christian, he or she has received the Holy Spirit, whose task and mandate is to fulfill the law of God in the lives of his people. The Holy Spirit will not be thwarted in his pursuit of that goal: he who has begun a good work within you will bring it to completion on the day of Christ Jesus (Phil. 1:6). Indeed, that good work will often be surprisingly fulfilled in the meantime: change and development are a common feature of the Christian life, thanks to the outpouring of the Spirit. Praise God for that! Pray for the outworking of that purpose in your own life and the lives of others, even while understanding that God changes each of us in his own way and according to his own timetable, not as we think he should. So look expectantly for his work in yourself and in others. Pray that by his Holy Spirit, God would continue to convict all of us of our sins and give us the grace to see Christ at work increasingly in every area of our lives. Ask that God would use you as an agent of positive change in the lives of those with whom you have contact: that he would teach you how to stir others up to love and good deeds (Heb. 10:24) while helping you stay patient with the often-slow tempo of the Spirit's work and your frequent stumbles into sin.

Second, Pentecost also reminds us that no Christian is above the need for ongoing, Holy Spirit–inspired change. Without the Holy Spirit, poured out at Pentecost, Israel's case really was hopeless, and even with the Holy Spirit, the apostles continued to struggle with sin in many ways. The apostle Peter was at the very center of the life-changing experience of that first Pentecost, yet he still needed other believers to confront him over his sin. Years later in Antioch, Peter was influenced by a group in the church who believed that Jewish Christians needed to observe all the Old Testament dietary laws in order to be saved; he therefore stopped eating with Gentile believers. Paul had to tell Peter that he was not living in line with the gospel (Gal. 2:11–14). If Peter himself could be so confused about something so foundational to the gospel, something God revealed to him personally in a divine vision (see Acts 10:10–48), how much more might that be true of the rest of us? We are all still works in progress, people in need of profound change, and we will be until we die. The Holy Spirit is not done with us yet, and he never will be this side of heaven.

We should certainly expect to see significant life change as the Holy Spirit does his work. But at the same time, part of the ongoing work of the Holy Spirit is to show us areas of our lives where the work is not done yet, to leave us with a holy dissatisfaction that drives us to see afresh our need for the free grace of Christ and the power of the Holy Spirit. The Spirit is sovereign over the agenda of our change: sometimes his agenda is to transform us by his power to enable new acts of obedience, while at other times it is to show us our utter inability to change ourselves. In those times of frustrating inability, God humbles us by revealing our weakness, thereby equipping us to come alongside others in their weakness and encourage them to find fresh hope in the gospel message of a righteousness outside ourselves, given to us as a free gift. When our sin drives us again to the cross to ask for mercy and to the throne of grace to plead for a greater outpouring of God's Spirit into our hearts, then we may be sure that the Holy Spirit is at work, for he delights to magnify Christ and the gospel.

The Spirit and the Beginning of the Harvest

Pentecost was and is more than simply a celebration of the giving of the law and, in Christ, of God's gift of a new righteousness. Pentecost was also, most importantly, a harvest festival. That was the central motif of the Feast of Weeks: it was the festival of the grain harvest, and on Pentecost each year two loaves of the firstfruits were taken to the temple to be elevated in the presence of the Lord as an acknowledgment of the God from whom all good gifts come (Lev. 23:17). In a similar way, the pouring out of the Spirit on that first Pentecost was the firstfruits of the great harvest of the kingdom of God. Three thousand people responded to Peter's preaching that day (Acts 2:41). It was the start of a harvest that has never ceased since; it was the bringing of men, women, and children from every tribe and nation under heaven into the kingdom of God.

That is what Luke dwells on as the key significance of the day of Pentecost. He describes three dramatic phenomena that took place on that day: violent wind, tongues of fire, and the ability to speak other languages (Acts 2:2–4). However, it is the last of these phenomena on which Luke dwells because it is the last that gives the apostles power to witness. Such power is the primary mark of the coming of the Holy Spirit into someone's life in the book of Acts (1:8). Yes, when the Spirit comes, he gives power—he is the Spirit of the all-powerful God. Yes, when the Spirit comes, he brings purity—he is, after all, the *Holy* Spirit. But what Luke focuses on in his account is not power or purity as such, but specifically the power to witness. The disciples had been gathered together praying for the Holy Spirit to be poured out, and he was—with the immediate result that they were given power to witness to the crowds about Jesus.

That's the real significance of this incident of what is sometimes called "speaking in tongues" (2:6). This event is radically different from what our charismatic brothers and sisters mean by speaking in tongues. The charismatic experience of speaking in tongues is nearly always an experience of unintelligible speech: even in their own view, it cannot be understood unless someone interprets it. What happened on the day of Pentecost, however, was unique and entirely different—almost the exact opposite of the charismatic experience, in fact. On that day the entire crowd, gathered from all parts of the Roman Empire, heard the message about Jesus in their own languages (2:6). The whole point of Pentecost is that there was no need for any interpreter! Everyone heard the gospel proclaimed in his or her own dialect.

What is so amazing about this phenomenon is that in a sense, it was entirely unnecessary. After all, a language already existed in which the apostles could easily have made themselves known to the vast majority of their hearers: Greek. The apostles managed perfectly well preaching in Greek elsewhere in the book of Acts. So it wasn't simply the necessity of making their message understandable that the Holy Spirit accomplished by enabling them to speak these multiple human languages. It was much more than that. What we see here is nothing less than a symbolic reversal of the events of the Tower of Babel. In Genesis 11:1–9, mankind in its arrogance decided to build a tower that would reach up to heaven—the Tower of Babel. But God put a stop to the people's proud efforts by confusing their languages so that they could no longer work together. Here on the first day of the church's mission to the world, an important precedent was being set. Many of the nations that are described here are the same as those that were scattered in the Table of Nations in Genesis 10,[3] but here they are gathered together in Jerusalem to hear the gospel in their own languages and dialects, in ways that are appropriate to their own cultures. Man's proud tower will never reach heaven to force his way back into God's presence; but at Pentecost, heaven came down to earth to redeem people from every culture.

Pentecost and Human Cultures

Pentecost tells us that our worship and preaching has to be in the language of the people. We want people who visit a church service who

3 See P. S. Alexander, "Geography and the Bible [Early Jewish]," in *Anchor Yale Bible Dictionary*, vol. 2, ed. David Noel Freedman (Yale University Press, 1992), 983.

are not yet Christians to be able to understand what we are talking about without having to take a preliminary course in church jargon (1 Cor. 14:23–25). It also tells us that our churches should reflect the culture of the people who make them up. There is no single cultural blueprint for the church. A church in California should feel different from a church in New England, let alone from a church in New Delhi. That doesn't mean our worship is to be driven by the lowest common denominator of whatever people in our area happen to like. The gospel critiques and challenges aspects of each culture just as it affirms aspects of every culture. But our worship must be comprehensible to all; it must not put unnecessary obstacles in the way of anyone.

To me, this is one of the tremendous benefits of the Presbyterian system of church government: a church is free at the local level to fit into its local culture, while on a larger scale it can be part of something that is profoundly multicultural. A Black church should be free to reflect Black culture in its worship, a messianic church to reflect Jewish culture, and a Rust Belt church to reflect working-class culture while recognizing that in Christ there is neither black nor white, Jew nor Gentile, rich nor poor (Gal. 3:28). It requires abundant grace and hard work to prevent our cultural differences from driving us apart into denominations that are functionally segregated by race, social class, and age group, but it is a challenge we need to face up to.

So the coming of the Holy Spirit gave the apostles power to speak in a culturally relevant way into the lives of all who heard them that first Pentecost: everyone heard them speak in his or her own dialect. Moreover, because the Holy Spirit was at work, a great harvest was reaped. Three thousand people from diverse backgrounds became Christians and were baptized into the church (Acts 2:41). The Holy Spirit gave power to witness, not just to a specially selected few preachers but to all the believers: "And they were all filled with the Holy Spirit and began to speak in other tongues as the Spirit gave them utterance" (2:4). This is another mark of the new era of the pouring out of the Spirit: In the Old Testament, the Spirit was given to a few specific individuals to empower them for specific tasks. Now he is poured out on all the believers to empower them for this one task of the church: being witnesses to Jesus Christ in Jerusalem, in all Judea, in Samaria, and to the ends of the earth (see Acts 1:8).

Witnesses for Christ

In this Spirit-filled empowering, nobody was left out. No one had to pray for a second blessing. Nobody left it to the professionals. All became the prophets of the Lord. We sometimes speak of the priesthood of all believers—the fact that all believers have equal access to God through Christ, the fact that we don't need a special class of intermediaries anymore to go into God's presence for us. But we should also speak of the "prophethood" of all believers. All Christians share in the task of making known to the nations what God has done in Jesus Christ through the power of the Spirit. That is a key aspect of what it means to be a prophet. A prophet is an ambassador: a person who knows God and is empowered by the Holy Spirit with a message from God for the world. Since the coming of the Spirit on the church that first Pentecost, the words *prophet* and *ambassador* describe each one of us. We should pray, therefore, that the same Holy Spirit would open doors for us also to be bold witnesses for Jesus to our families, friends, and neighbors.

In a foreshadowing of the skeptical response that the gospel will encounter later in the book of Acts, some responded to God's remarkable work on that first Pentecost by asserting that the apostles were merely drunk (Acts 2:13), though this could hardly account for their sudden ability to speak in many languages that they had not studied! This response gave Peter the opportunity to explain the miraculous sign to them in terms of the words of the prophet Joel (Acts 2:14–21; Joel 2:28–32). These events were not random phenomena stemming from drunkenness but were instead a fulfillment of Old Testament prophecy. Indeed, Peter's boldness to speak to the large crowd that had gathered was itself a mark of the difference the pouring out of the Spirit had made: Earlier, he had been too timid to confess his allegiance to Christ in private to a serving girl (Luke 22:56–58), but now he was willing to preach Christ to any who would listen.

The reality that the Spirit of God has now been poured out on all of us, male and female, young and old, wealthy and poor, should also shape our prayers. Don't simply pray for God's Spirit to be poured out on your neighbors so that they will come to church; pray for God's Spirit to be poured out on the church so that we will go out in the power of the Holy Spirit to bring the message of Jesus Christ to those around us. That is what happens to the believers on the day of Pentecost. The Holy Spirit fills them with power and sends them out, and as they preach the good news about Jesus they find that the Holy Spirit has gone ahead of them, opening up the hearts of some of their hearers to receive the message. Yes, you can and should pray for God to open people's hearts through the Holy Spirit—but don't forget to pray that the Holy Spirit might be poured out on you too, to give you power to witness to Christ. Pray for opportunities to speak clearly for Christ to your existing network of friends and relations, as well as to total strangers whom the Spirit brings to you.

Our Message

Our message is Jesus Christ: God in human flesh, who kept the law for us, died on the cross in our place, was raised up on the third day from the dead, and has now been exalted into heaven, where he sits at the Father's right hand. The Spirit always lifts up and glorifies Christ, and so should we. His perfect life substitutes for all our many failures. His death in our place atones for our many sins. In him we become God's children and are brought into a glorious inheritance in company with all the other saints, whom he delights to call his own people.

Not everybody will welcome our message, to be sure. There will always be those who ridicule God's witnesses, just as there were on the day of Pentecost, when some advanced the ludicrous suggestion that the apostles were drunk (Acts 2:13). But there is a harvest to be reaped today also, a harvest of men and women who will turn from depending on their own efforts and righteousness, and trust instead in what Jesus Christ has done for them. As we go out in the power of the Holy Spirit, the living God will draw them in and establish vibrant communities of Christians who worship and serve him in ways that reflect and are appropriate to their own cultures. The presence of the Holy Spirit may ebb and flow with his people, and it is appropriate that we should pray for him to be poured out in greater measure. But fundamentally the message of Pentecost is this: The Holy Spirit has now been poured out; you have received power from on high. Now we are called to go and, as God enables us, use that power to be God's witnesses locally and throughout the world, bringing in the full harvest of which Pentecost was the firstfruits.

4

The Heart of the Good News

Acts 2:22–41

SUPPOSE SOMEONE were to come up to you this week and say, "I've heard that you're a Christian. There's something about you Christians that is different, and I want to know what it is. Tell me what has made such a difference in your life." That would be a wonderful opportunity, the kind of opening for which we all long and pray. And that's exactly the situation in which Peter finds himself on the day of Pentecost. The interest of the crowd has been stirred by an astonishing miracle in which many different people, gathered from many different lands, have heard the young church speaking to them in their own dialects (Acts 2:6). Now Peter has the opportunity to speak to the crowd and explain exactly what is happening in front of their eyes.

You and I may never have the opportunity to address such large crowds, but we will undoubtedly have opportunities in the course of daily life to share our faith in Jesus Christ with others. We can learn what lies at the heart of Christianity from Peter's sermon, the very first sermon given in the new church in Jerusalem.

Rooted in History

Peter starts his message by focusing our attention on a sequence of historical events that are recorded for us in the Gospels of the New

Testament. According to Peter, the key facts are these: Jesus was a man whose authorization by God was made abundantly clear by the miracles that he did, miracles that were such public knowledge that they could not possibly be denied (Acts 2:22). Immediately Peter exposes several popular contemporary misunderstandings of who Jesus is. For example, he makes no mention of Jesus being a good teacher or a fine moral example for us to pattern our lives after. Jesus was both of those things, but they were not what was central to his ministry or Peter would have mentioned them. Equally, Peter is eager to put to rest the idea that Jesus was a fraud. He is willing to challenge a potentially hostile audience to deny that Jesus did great miracles. Jesus's ministry had been marked by so many miracles, and those miracles had been so widely attested that no one could deny that they had happened. Nor were these miracles simply random party tricks; they were signs that God himself was at work in the ministry of Jesus. Peter starts his Pentecost sermon, then, by asserting the uniqueness of Jesus: Jesus was a man whose message was authorized by God through dramatic signs.

Indeed, the events of the day of Pentecost were themselves one more sign authorizing the ministry of Jesus. This pouring out of the Spirit on all God's people, longed for by Moses in Numbers 11 and prophesied by Joel in Joel 2, has happened in front of their eyes, because this same Jesus has now ascended to the right hand of the Father. Jesus, the promised Messiah, was the one who poured out the promised Spirit of God on the church, as they have just witnessed (Acts 2:33).

Second, Peter moves on to identify the death and resurrection of Jesus as the central events of his ministry here on earth (2:23–24). This is a truly remarkable claim. Most religions claim that the life and teaching of their founder was of great significance for the world. Muslims claim that the life and teaching of Mohammed is a key turning point in the history of humanity, while Mormons claim the same honor for Joseph Smith. Of course the life of Jesus Christ was important, as was his teaching. Luke spends considerable effort documenting that life and teaching in his gospel. However, Christians are unique in claiming that the *death* of Jesus Christ was the crucial event that changed the course of world history forever.

This is a particularly remarkable claim given the nature of Christ's death: execution by crucifixion, a form of torture that the Romans reserved for the worst criminals and terrorists and that the Jews regarded as a sign of a person who stood under God's judgment (Deut. 21:22–23). Yet according to Peter, Christ's violent and painful death was not a tragic accident of fate or a miscalculation on the part of heaven, a failure to predict just how evil humans could be to one another. Rather, that death on the cross was at the very same time both the sinful act of wicked men and part of God's perfect plan to rescue his people (Acts 2:23).

It was certainly wicked to crucify the only perfect person the world has ever known. There is no excusing of sin here. Yet even this epitome of evil, this height and depth of Satan's raging against goodness and light, was not for an instant outside heaven's control. God didn't hand over his Son to men with bated breath, waiting to see what they would do with him. He knew already that they would beat his Son cruelly and hammer nails through the palms of his hands and the soles of his feet, leaving him gasping on a cross of wood until he died an excruciating death. What is more, Peter says that God the Father actually willed that awful fate for his dearly beloved Son and that Jesus willingly undertook its agony, receiving its cup of suffering and a curse from his Father's hand (Acts 2:23). The crucifixion was not simply the natural response of evil men to ultimate goodness; it was at the exact same time the willing and sovereign choice of ultimate goodness to receive an undeserved curse. God allows many things to happen in this world that are genuinely evil while at the same time accomplishing through them his own good and holy purposes to bless his people (Rom. 8:28).

The Necessity of the Cross and the Resurrection

Why would anyone willingly subject himself to such a fate as a crucifixion? Who would ask their beloved Son to take upon himself such an awful death? It is one thing to endure undeserved suffering stoically when it is out of your control, but it is quite another to seek out and embrace suffering deliberately on behalf of another. Why would God himself, who has the power to accomplish everything he desires, deliberately choose to go to the cross? The only possible answer to the question is that the cross must have been absolutely necessary as the only way to achieve an even more precious goal—namely, the salvation of God's people.[1] This immediately rules out the idea that the cross is simply a way for Jesus to show us just how much he loves us. To make a necessary sacrifice for love is noble; to make an unnecessary sacrifice of your life is not noble—it is pathological. For example, if while we are walking together along the road I see a runaway car approaching and I push you out of the way at the cost of my own life, that is heroic. However, if I simply say to you, "Look how much I love you!" and then throw myself under a passing car when you are in no danger, there is nothing noble about my gesture. It is a sign of a serious psychiatric disorder. In other words, the cross becomes a symbol of the Father and the Son's love for their people only if it was absolutely necessary—if there were absolutely no other way in which God's people could be redeemed.

But why was the cross necessary? How is this death different from so many other tragic endings in a world that is filled with a great deal of unjust suffering and undeserved death? The answer is this: because of our sinful rebellion against God, we all deserve to die—not just physically but spiritually. The prophet Isaiah tells us that all of us humans have gone our own way like sheep and have broken the laws of the Maker of the universe in ways that are small and large (Isa. 53:6). The apostle Paul sums it up like this: "All have sinned and fallen short of the glory of God" (Rom. 3:23). He goes on to tell us that the wages that such rebellion merits are nothing less than death itself. Left to ourselves, we all deserve eternal separation from the one whose presence is meaning and light but whose directions we have scorned. Instead of loving our God and our neighbors, as we were made to do, we have all turned our backs on our Creator and hated those made in his image in our thoughts, words, and deeds.

1 See John Murray, *Redemption Accomplished and Applied* (Eerdmans, 1955), 12.

But at the cross, we were not left to ourselves. God himself entered our broken world and our broken lives to rescue us from ourselves. By enduring the agony of the cross, Christ took into himself our deserved fate of isolation and lostness. He suffered a fate that he didn't deserve in order to free us from the fate that we richly deserved—and there was no other way that we could have been freed. The cross makes it abundantly clear that our best efforts to merit salvation could never have done the trick. None of us can live up to God's standard of perfection and keep every aspect of his holy law.

The good news of the gospel, however, is that Jesus didn't stay dead. The central act of world history is not merely the death of Christ; it is the death plus the resurrection of Christ. The verdict of man on him, "This man shall die," was reversed in a higher court—in the highest court of all—and Jesus Christ was raised up from the dead (Acts 2:24). It was not possible for death to hold Jesus, for he had no sin; he always loved and obeyed his Father in thought, word, and deed. Not only that, Jesus has now been exalted to the right hand of God the Father in heaven and has poured out the Holy Spirit on the church (2:33).

The evidence of that reality is the miracle that the people have all just seen and heard at Pentecost, which proved beyond a shadow of a doubt that Jesus Christ's sacrifice has been accepted by the Father. The plan of the Father and the Son to redeem a people for themselves has succeeded.

These events are what we as Christians celebrate, not merely once a year at Easter but Sunday after Sunday. Indeed, the day of our worship moved from the Old Testament Sabbath, Saturday, to the New Testament Sabbath, Sunday, precisely because Sunday is Resurrection Day—the day of the week when Christ rose from the dead. Every Sunday is now for us a celebration of the death and resurrection of Christ.

Two Witnesses

Peter then offers his hearers two convincing strands of testimony to support the events that he has just described. The first witness is the Old Testament. He points to passages in the Psalms that speak prophetically about the resurrection and ascension of Jesus. In Psalm 16, David declared his confidence that the Lord would not abandon his soul to destruction or let his flesh decay, while in Psalm 110 David spoke of someone greater than he who would be seated at the Lord's right hand until all his enemies were utterly subdued. Neither of these passages, says Peter, were fulfilled in the life of David or his offspring. As a matter of fact, David's rotting bones were buried not far from where Peter was speaking (Acts 2:29), while none of his heirs reigned over the entire world, or anything close to it. Rather, according to Peter, both passages describe the situation of David's greater descendant, Jesus, whose bones are now no longer in the tomb where they had been laid only a few weeks earlier. Unlike David, whose body remained lastingly entombed in death, Jesus has risen from the dead and ascended on high, where he is now seated at the right hand of the Father in glory. As Luke repeatedly reminds us, what the Old Testament anticipated, Jesus fulfilled.

The second testimony that Peter offers is the witness of the apostles: In verse 32, he declares that "we all are witnesses" to the fact of the resurrection. Peter and the other apostles have seen the risen Christ with their own eyes, and they testify to what they have seen, even though it will lead to intense suffering and, in virtually every case, their martyrdom for the faith. We as Christians today believe what we believe about Jesus Christ on the basis of exactly the same two strands of testimony that Peter offers: the Old Testament, which points forward to Christ, and the New Testament, which records the eyewitness testimony of the apostles to Christ. This is itself the work of the Spirit, opening our hearts and minds to the truth of the Scriptures.

The Scriptures are thus the objective basis for our Christian beliefs. We are not free to say, "I like to think of God as . . . ," and make up a God of our own imagining. We cannot shape our definitions of right or wrong to suit what our culture believes to be self-evident. Nor may we base our beliefs about Jesus ultimately on our own personal experience of him. We shouldn't say to people, as one hymnwriter did, "You ask me how I know he lives? He lives within my heart."[2] No, Christians be-

2 Alfred H. Ackley, "He Lives," 1933, https://www.hymnologyarchive.com/.

lieve in the Jesus whom they read about in the Bible, the Jesus whom the apostles saw rise from the dead with their own eyes. You ask me how I know he lives? The eyewitness accounts tell me so.

That is not to say that Christians don't have a personal experience of Jesus; of course we do. But fundamental to our belief structure is not what I feel about God or what my personal experience of the divine is but what God has revealed about himself in the Bible. We believe on the basis of the testimony of the Old and New Testaments, not on the basis of the testimony of a feeling in our hearts. Likewise, it is important that when we share our faith with people we make it clear that the reason we believe what we do is not that we happen to find these doctrines appealing or because of some unique personal experience we have had but rather because we find these doctrines in the Bible, which we believe to be God's word on the basis of its own compelling testimony.

That is important because many of us have been taught that to share the gospel means sharing your personal testimony: explaining to others your personal experience of the difference Jesus has made in your life. "Here's what a mess my life used to be; here's what a together person I am now. Jesus made the difference—so why don't you try Jesus too?" Strikingly, that isn't how the apostles shared the gospel. Peter didn't appeal to how timid and scared he used to be before he met Jesus and how Jesus helped him be bold enough to speak before thousands. Paul doesn't talk about how he used to be an angry and proud Pharisee but now that he is a Christian he has become much more gentle and loving. Undoubtedly, Peter and Paul had powerful personal testimonies—far more powerful than ours, most likely! Yet when someone asked them to share the gospel, they went repeatedly to the Scriptures of the Old Testament and to the eyewitness testimony of the apostles to prove that Jesus Christ is indeed risen from the dead.

The strength and weakness of personal testimonies is, of course, the fact that they are personal. As a result, it is easy for people to respond, "That's wonderful. I'm so glad that this Christianity business is working for you; obviously, you need some kind of emotional crutch to get through the week. But it's just not my thing." Authentic gospel proclamation won't let you off the hook quite so easily. It declares that we don't believe in Christianity because of what it does for us; rather, we believe in Christianity because it is true, and here are the witnesses who testify to it. Were they deluded? Were they deceivers? Or were they speaking the truth?

Cut to the Heart

You can see the impact of such preaching in the conclusion to Peter's sermon. Jesus told the disciples earlier that when the Holy Spirit came, he would give them power to witness about him, and now we see that promise being fulfilled. The people who hear Peter speak do not walk away at the end shaking his hand, saying, "Nice sermon, pastor." Instead, they are "cut to the heart" and cry out, "What shall we do?" (Acts 2:37). Peter's sermon, in the power of the Holy Spirit, moves people's hearts and brings them to the point where they know that they can no longer go on living the way they previously have. They understand they are guilty before God of condemning Jesus to death. Whether they were in the crowd actively crying out for his crucifixion or whether they have simply lived their lives according to their own best efforts, they understand that, either way, they are the reason Jesus Christ had to die. They are complicit in putting to death the Son of God. How can they escape so great a crime?

Perhaps you find yourself in that situation today. The Holy Spirit has been working in your heart to the point where you are aware of your own sinfulness but don't know what to do. Maybe you've done something in your past that is so awful that you wouldn't dare tell your best friend about it. Or perhaps you've never done anything very bad in the eyes of other people, but you know there is more than enough in your own thoughts to condemn you. Is it worse to rebel loudly and openly against God than to commit secret treason against him in your heart? To yell, "Crucify him," as you pound the nails into his hands or to mutter, "Nice sermon, pastor," while regarding Jesus and his costly sacrifice as a vague irrelevance to the real issues of your life? You need to join the crowd in Peter's day and cry out, "What must I do to be saved?"

Peter then lays out the conditions that come attached to God's free offer of salvation. Jesus Christ has paid for everything through his death on the cross. You can't add anything to his payment. You don't need to straighten out your life before you come to him; you can only come as you are. But when you come to Jesus, you need to come with a repentant heart, resigning your right to decide for yourself how you will live or what things are right and wrong, resigning your pride and your self-sufficiency, sorrowing over your many sins. Salvation is free, but it can be received only by those who come with empty hands, casting away any dependence on themselves or anything else apart from Jesus Christ.

United with Christ

You can see what repentance looked like for Peter's first hearers in his command for them to be baptized (Acts 2:38). The Jews believed that baptism was for the most part for Gentile converts, not for Jews or their children. They had circumcision: that was how they proved their standing before God. So for a Jew to come and be baptized into the name of the very one that they had rejected and crucified would be a clear public token of their repentance. They would be demonstrating that they no longer wanted to be seen as standing before God in their own righteousness as Jews but in the righteousness of Jesus Christ into whose name they are baptized. They have moved from one community into another: now they are part of the community of those who believe in Jesus. Therefore, they could expect to receive the promises that were made to those who are part of that community: the forgiveness of their sins, the gift of Christ's righteousness, and the gift of the Holy Spirit. It is not as if baptism magically confers those blessings on them. Rather, it symbolizes the necessary repentance in their hearts as well as the necessity of the Holy Spirit at work in their hearts, who regenerated them and made them new creatures in Christ.

If you are to cease to identify with the world and become part of God's people in Christ, there may be some particular sin or lifestyle choice that you know you would have to give up. Maybe you need to give up trusting in your own wisdom or in your belief that your life is good enough that God ought to accept you on the basis of it. Baptism symbolizes your need to become like a helpless little child and be washed clean by God; it points to a renewal of your heart by the Holy Spirit that you cannot accomplish for yourself (Ezek. 36:25–27).

Repentance is not merely the entry point into the Christian life; it is, as Martin Luther said in the first of his ninety-five theses, the hallmark of every stage of the Christian life.[3] It is not as if we repent once, acknowledging our inability to please God by ourselves, and God then gives us the power to keep his law. Sometimes we are tempted to believe that since Christians have the Spirit within us we ought to be able to live lives of profound holiness. But that is a spiritual form of the health and wealth gospel: it is to believe that what God has promised us in heaven can be completely attained here on earth. Of course, we should pursue holiness with a passion. Our God has loved us and given us his own Son, and his ultimate will for us is perfect holiness, which is for our good as well as for his glory. Why wouldn't we want what he wants? But as long as we remain here on earth, we remain weak, struggling believers who daily need to hear God's call to repent afresh. As we do, we need to return repeatedly to the heart of the gospel that Peter lays out here.

For it remains gloriously true that this Jesus whom we crucified and killed through our sinful acts, just as surely as if we personally took up the hammer and nails on Golgotha, is still the one whom God attested as his own Son. He died not just because we killed him but because the triune God himself—Father, Son, and Holy Spirit—had chosen to have a people for himself and by his grace paid the full penalty for our present and future sin, as well as for our past sin. This same Jesus also rose from the dead and is now seated at the Father's right hand, where he continues to be at work in us by the Holy Spirit. That means that if you belong to him, then your life is one in which the risen Christ continues to be active by his Holy Spirit, poured out on that first Pentecost. He is

3 Martin Luther, *Martin Luther's Ninety-Five Theses*, ed. Stephen J. Nichols (P&R, 2002), 23.

the one who cut you to the heart in the first place so that you came to trust in him. He will continue to cut you to the heart regularly, showing you more of your sinfulness and your need for the gospel, sometimes in small ways and at other times in large ways.

The Continuing Work of the Holy Spirit

When Christians talk about being filled with the Spirit as those first believers were at Pentecost, we often have in mind sharing the strange phenomena of the earlier verses. We expect to be filled with power to triumph over our adversaries. Yet we are often less enthusiastic about the other work of the Holy Spirit at Pentecost: convicting people of their sins and showing them their desperate need for Christ. It is certainly true that, at times, the Holy Spirit will enable you to stand boldly by his gracious power, to show you the difference he is able to make in your life. In those moments you will need to look back to your baptism and remind yourself that this is nothing you have done; it is the fruit of God's gift of the Holy Spirit to give you a new heart, a heart of flesh in place of your old stony heart (Ezek. 36:26). At other times, the Holy Spirit will let you fall flat on your face and cut you to your heart, showing you how little power you have in yourself, even as a Christian. At times like that, you will need to look back to your baptism and remind yourself that God has marked you out as belonging to him and he will not let you go. Christ's righteousness is enough for you, weak as you are.

There will be times when evil people conspire against you in little or large ways, and you will be tempted to doubt God's care for you. Yet the God who planned and orchestrated such a costly salvation for your soul has not left the rest of your life unplanned. You are united to Christ, and nothing in all creation can separate you from your living Lord, who even now intercedes at the right hand of the Father for you. Not even the worst acts of the worst people can separate you from the love of Christ (Rom. 8:35–39). Even death itself cannot separate us from the love of God in Jesus Christ. We may commit the bones of the ones we love to earthly tombs, but Christ's resurrection speaks a better word for them too. Those who have trusted in Christ are not left to rot in a shadowy world of death and decay. They are even now in the presence of the Lord, delighting in his beauty and marveling at his love for lost humanity.

This is the heart of the good news about Jesus. This is what we believe, and this is what we have been called to declare repeatedly to ourselves, to our children, and to those who are still far off from Christ (Acts 2:39): "This Jesus whom you crucified" God has made Lord of lords and King of kings, and he reigns in heaven forever. So look back and see the proof of God's love for you in the cross. Look upward to the right hand of the Father and remind yourself that Jesus Christ still reigns, in the face of the evidence of your unruly heart, of your most chaotic and inexplicable life circumstances, and of the seeming triumph of evil forces on all sides. And then look onward to the day for which Jesus Christ is still waiting, the day when all his enemies will fully and finally be subdued under his feet. On that day, he will complete the good work that he has begun in you, and in this world, and he will reign forever and ever.

5

New Life, New Lifestyle

Acts 2:42–47

THERE'S SOMETHING DECIDEDLY odd about Christians. At least there ought to be. When Jesus Christ takes hold of you, there should be a change in your lifestyle that is so dramatic that people cannot explain you except by the fact that you are a Christian. When people look at the church, they should be puzzled. Outwardly, church people may seem like normal, ordinary, everyday folk. But when you look at what they do and how they live—well, you have to wonder! They are not like other people. In fact, they are distinctly odd! That was certainly the effect that the early church had on those around them: Luke says that everyone was filled with awe by them (Acts 2:43). The other inhabitants of Jerusalem were astonished at the change in these people. You couldn't explain it except by the fact that they were part of this new movement. They were Christians.

Devoted to the Apostles' Teaching

The first area in which the lives of the Christians of Acts 2 is remarkable is that they are "devoted . . . to the apostles' teaching" (Acts 2:42). They are committed to learning everything they can about God and about Jesus Christ. As a result, they are committed to learning at the feet of those who have been with Jesus, the apostles. They are eager to be taught—not just a brief snippet or two of information but everything Jesus did and everything he taught his disciples. This was, of course, the commission that Jesus had given the apostles in Matthew 28:20: they were to go and make disciples of all nations, baptizing them and "teaching them to observe all that I have commanded you." So it is perfectly natural that the apostles want to devote their time to teaching the people. But what is rather remarkable is that the people want to devote themselves to being taught. No one is saying after thirty minutes, "Time's up; I wish that the sermon were over." Instead, they say, "Teach us! Tell us everything that Jesus ever said. Help us understand the significance of the Old Testament. We just can't get enough of the truth about Christ."

That attitude is the work of the Holy Spirit. It is the Holy Spirit's job not simply to empower preachers but also to open up the hearts of those who hear with a hunger for the truth, for learning more about Jesus. In John 16:13, Jesus calls the Holy Spirit "the Spirit of truth" and tells his disciples that "when the Spirit of truth comes, he will guide you into all the truth." So when that same Holy Spirit is poured out at Pentecost (Acts 2:1–41), it is not surprising that people can't get enough of the apostles' teaching.

The same has happened down throughout church history whenever the Holy Spirit has come on the church in power. At the beginning of the Reformation, when the Swiss Reformer Ulrich Zwingli announced that he would preach daily from the Greek text of the Gospel of Matthew, crowds flocked to the Great Minster in Zurich to hear his simple and direct messages. When George Whitefield and John Wesley preached in the open air to working-class miners in England, or to crowds of colonists in America, there was a constant hunger for more. That's what happens whenever the Holy Spirit takes hold of a heart or a church or a community. There is a profound hunger for biblical truth and a desire to know God's word more deeply.

We have the same treasure house of the knowledge of God open to us in the pages of the Bible. In this precious book we have the very words of the apostles and prophets of God and those who heard them, written down inerrantly under the inspiration of God himself (2 Tim. 3:16). So we ought to be equally committed to learning about the will and ways of God from his word. How sad it would be if we had only a little hunger for the apostolic message! We should get down on our knees and plead with God to pour out his Spirit increasingly into our hearts so that we might increasingly hunger for his word. Without that work of the Spirit, we will have no hunger. What we need is not merely a natural taste for learning or the pursuit of knowledge. Rather, it is a divine gift that we should all long to have, for the Spirit never works without or apart from the word.

Committed to Doctrine

Now if you hunger for the apostolic teaching, the world will find that surprising on two counts. First, they will find it surprising that you are committed to doctrine. "Doctrine" is something of a dirty word in an age that hardly recognizes any dirty words at all. There are almost no words left that you could offend people with, but "doctrine" is one of the few that still has the capacity to shock. Whenever I planted a new church, people would say to me, "Why are you starting a new church? Why not get together with all the other churches? After all, don't you all believe basically the same things, whether you're Catholic, Methodist, Baptist, or Lutheran—not to mention all those different Presbyterian denominations?" And there is a sense in which that is true. Much of what we believe has been believed by all Christians at all times and in all places. That's why we can still recite the Apostles' Creed, though it was written many centuries ago. There are many other Christians in other denominations with whom we share a great deal of belief.

But what about the remaining areas? If we believe that the Bible instructs us about baptism, about the Lord's Supper, about the role of men and women in the church, about how believers grow in holiness, and about the centrality of the gospel in every area of life, and if we are committed to the apostles' teaching, then we cannot simply pass over these things as if they were unimportant. Yes, we must hold to our doctrinal formulations humbly, recognizing that not all Christians will agree with us; but we must also hold to them firmly because God would not have revealed these things in his word if they were not important. Just because real Christians disagree on any particular topic doesn't mean that there aren't right and wrong answers to the questions we ask about the Bible's teaching. Not everything in Scripture is open for endless debate. So we make it our duty and our joy to search the Scriptures on our own and with others, reading books and listening to sermons like the Bereans, seeking to establish whether or not these things are true (Acts 17:10–12). We ought to be utterly committed to doctrine.

The reality is that you can't actually escape being committed to doctrine. We all have beliefs, and those beliefs shape the way we interpret every experience that we have. Even the idea that doctrine is a nasty, divisive thing that we should ignore in favor of just loving Jesus is itself a doctrine—and not one that is in accord with God's word. The question is not whether you are going to be devoted to doctrine but whether you are constantly going to expose your doctrines to the searching light of God's word and let the apostolic teaching be the yardstick by which all your personal doctrines are measured. We are all driven by our doctrine; the only question is, What drives your doctrine: God's word or some other standard?

Committed to the Bible

The second thing that the world will find surprising about us in our commitment to apostolic doctrine is our commitment to the Bible. We've already mentioned that the Bible, the place in which we find the teaching of the apostles and prophets written down for us, is to be the source of our doctrine. A lot of people will find that commitment downright strange. When I lived in England, I was invited to do a "Thought for the Day" spot occasionally on BBC Radio Oxford. Once, while I was there to do my little piece, the producer of the morning show asked me what our church was about because she had no idea what a Presbyterian was. As I explained our commitment to God as our sovereign King and to his will revealed in his word, the Bible, I could see the look of incredulity growing on the face of this bright young woman. "You mean," she said, finally grasping the enormity of what I was saying, "you actually believe the Bible is true, not just a collection of meaningful myths?" It boggled her mind that there were still people like me around in the modern world. I don't know if I was really the first person she'd ever met who believed that the Bible was God's word, but my story proves my point. People will constantly be surprised that the source of what you believe is the Bible and that you really believe it.

It is not as if anyone functions without norms. None of us has invented our own belief system from scratch. We believe what we believe because of our culture or because our parents believed it or because our parents believed the opposite or because we think science tells us so or whatever. We all have norms against which we test our various beliefs. Christians are unusual, however, in that we are very explicit about our norming norm: the Scriptures shape our beliefs and our practices in a way that allows us to be self-conscious and reflective about our lives.

Devoted to Fellowship

The second mark of the early Christian church was their fellowship. "And day by day, attending the temple together and breaking bread in their homes, they received their food with glad and generous hearts" (Acts 2:46). The word translated "fellowship" back in Acts 2:42 means "close association involving mutual interests and sharing."[1] As Christians, we automatically have a lot in common. We share a common heavenly Father and so we are part of the same family. We share a common faith and so we are going to spend eternity together. It should be natural to us that we behave as a family right now.

A healthy family has certain common characteristics. It should be a place that is rich in unconditional welcome, rich in close relationships, and rich in sacrificial giving. It doesn't matter whether you are Black or Hispanic or Asian or White, prosperous or poor, educated or

1 Frederick W. Danker, Walter Bauer, William D. Arndt, and F. Wilbur Gingrich, *A Greek-English Lexicon of the New Testament and Other Early Christian Literature*, 3rd ed. (University of Chicago Press, 2000), 552.

uneducated, man or woman, Republican or Democrat; you should find a welcome in the church. If you are a believer in Christ, then you are my brother or sister. This is something that you see when you travel around the world. Wherever you go, you find a warm and immediate welcome in the church. When I was an undergraduate engineering student, I spent a summer in South Africa working in a gold mine. There were five of us students from the UK who were assigned to this particular mine, and two of us were Christians. The first Sunday, we went to the local church and were welcomed warmly. Because we were Christians, we were automatically part of their family. We spent most of our free time during those eight weeks at the homes of church members and had a great time. The other three students were bored out of their minds, continually complaining that there was nothing to do in this one-horse town!

That unconditional welcome isn't always as easy as it sounds. We are programmed to rate people's value based on what they can do for us. Do these people eat on the "cool" side of the cafeteria? Are they able to entertain me with witty conversation? Do they like the things I like? Are they at the same stage of life that I am at? We are by nature people users, whose first thought when we enter a room is "Where are the people who will make me feel and look good?" In the gospel, however, that thought is turned upside down. Now, for the first time, as we follow Christ, we start to become people servers. After church your first thought should be, "Who is standing by herself? Who doesn't have a group of people already gathered around him? Who can I serve by lovingly taking the time to talk to her and find out what's going on in her life?" After all, these people are family.

But it is not just the fact that we are natural people users that blocks us from having fellowship with one another. It is also the fact that we are profoundly broken people who often sin against each other and then aren't sure what to do next. We offend one another in word and deed, and the result is broken fellowship. The good news of our unconditional acceptance in Christ, however, gives us the boldness to step out and try to restore broken fellowship. The gospel grounds our hearts in the forgiveness that we have received from God, which then enables us to begin to go and show similar forgiveness to those around us, and to repent and ask for forgiveness from those we have offended.

In our society, we have a consistent impulse to hide our sin, or to explain it away, in order to pretend that "I'm okay and you're okay." That attitude shuts down any possibility of real relationship. Real relationships require honesty and openness; only fake intimacy can be achieved in a relationship where we pretend there is nothing wrong with us, and nothing wrong with the other person either. On the contrary, the gospel allows us to confess to one another that I'm actually not okay and you're not okay either—but through the righteousness of Christ, God has made a way for each of us to be reckoned righteous before him (2 Cor. 5:21). My standing before God rests on his righteousness, not my own. This provides the foundation for deep and lasting relationships, relationships that can endure the alienation that sin causes, by means of repentance and restoration to friendship with God and with one another.

A family should also be a place that is rich in close relationships. In these days when people are scattered far away from their relatives, it is hard for your family to be your best friends. Many—perhaps most—of us are a long way from home. As a result, many people around us lead lives that are barren of close friendships. Loneliness is a fact of life in our modern world. We don't have any family members close enough to invite over on the spur of the moment, so who will be family to us? The answer is that church should be our family. You don't have to wait for the church to organize these "family gatherings" either. Call someone you don't know very well and arrange to have lunch or dinner with that person; take the opportunity to be family to him or her. What is more, because this is family, your in-person fellowship doesn't necessarily have to be tidy or peaceful. It doesn't have to be a gourmet meal on fine china; it can be spaghetti and meatballs on paper plates. It can be a cup of espresso at a coffee shop. It can be a game of catch or a walk together down by the river. As we spend time together, we grow together as the family of God, building rich relationships together. The church father Tertullian wrote that outsiders said of the early church, "See how these Christians love one another!"[2] The same should be their response today.

Sacrificial Giving

Family is also meant to be a place of sacrificial giving. One of the saddest aspects of modern family life is that this dimension has been almost totally removed from the expectations people have for the family. Now people enter relationships largely in order to fulfill themselves, and they reserve the right to bail out if their needs are not being met. That is why there has been such a rise in couples living together. "We've got to find out if we're compatible," they say. Is compatibility so desperately important? Yes it is, if you are using the relationship to fulfill yourself. But what if marriage is not primarily about fulfilling yourself? What if it is about sacrificing yourself to minister to your spouse, about the husband loving the wife as Christ loved the church? Does your spouse always fulfill you? No. Are there tensions? Yes. And that is true in every marriage. But in the Christian marriage, there is the commitment that, no matter what, you give yourself to your spouse completely, utterly, sacrificially.

It has to be that way in a healthy marriage because when children come along you don't have a choice. Little babies are not compatible with a normal lifestyle. They call for sacrificial giving—and not just some of the time but constantly. Their mothers (and hopefully their fathers too) give again and again and again—right up until they pay for college tuition and a wedding. As Barb and I have discovered now that our kids have grown up, you still sacrifice for them even beyond those events. But as they grow up, the children also begin to learn to give sacrificially to one another. Nothing gladdens a parent's heart like the sight of one child freely and spontaneously sharing their toys with another. Or when one sibling loses her job and the other siblings call her up to pray with her and help her through this challenging time.

2 Tertullian, *Apology*, in Tertullian, Minucius Felix, *Apology. De Spectaculis. Minucius Felix: Octavius*, trans. T. R. Glover and Gerald H. Rendall, Loeb Classical Library 250 (Harvard University Press, 1931), 177.

Self-sacrificial giving is what being family is all about. But the world will find it utterly astonishing. We even find the New Testament believers selling their possessions in order to meet the needs of others (Acts 2:44) because their hearts were overcome by grace and they couldn't bear to see other brothers and sisters in Christ destitute and in need. This self-sacrificial giving is not simply about caring for one another in financial ways, though that is obviously included. It means coming alongside one another and practically caring for others in a multitude of different ways. Ask yourself: What can I do for someone else in the church this week to show that I care about them? How can I practically demonstrate the love of Christ by sharing something with which I have been abundantly blessed? It could be as simple as helping someone paint their living room or offering to babysit free of charge or giving people without a car a ride to the doctor's office. Whatever shape it takes, self-sacrificial giving flows from the same root: we care for one another because we are family.

Excelling in the Grace of Giving

What about those who are believers in other parts of the world who don't have enough to buy food? What can we do for them? We are part of God's family throughout the world. Every church exists in part because of the sacrificial giving of Christians elsewhere; so, too, we want to be able to take our part in blessing others with the riches God has given us as we give sacrificially for his work. In the Old Testament, God's people were commanded to give a tithe to the poor (Deut. 26:12); I don't believe that as Christians we are under that same legal obligation to tithe.[3] But should we, who have experienced God's grace so much more richly than Old Testament believers had, give less than they? I'm not suggesting that we should be legalistic about a figure of 10 percent. The gracious giving of sacrificial love is not constantly calculating the cost. Sometimes it may give much more; sometimes

3 Iain M. Duguid, *Should Christians Tithe? Excelling in the Grace of Giving* (St. Colme's Press, 2018).

it may sorrowfully recognize that it cannot give that much right now. But sacrificial love delights to give, and give, and then give some more, rejoicing whenever it is able to meet the beloved's needs. This is what Paul means when he urges the Corinthians to "excel" in the grace of giving (2 Cor. 8:7).

This is a gift that I covet for the church. We ought to astound the people who live around us with a generosity that overflows to all in need, whether Christian or non-Christian. My Scottish forbears would say to me, "It's not practical." Love never is. You can't tell a young man who buys a diamond ring for his bride that giving is not practical. Of course it isn't; it's an outpouring of a heart on fire with love. The early church was on fire with love for Jesus, overflowing with joy over the grace they had received. And that overflow poured itself out in giving so generously that the needs of all were astonishingly met as some sold their property and possessions to fund it. Was it practical? No. Was it magnificent? Yes. Was it puzzling and convicting to all who saw it? Absolutely.

Committed to Worship and Prayer

Another surprising aspect of the early Christian community was that they were devoted to the breaking of bread and to prayer (Acts 2:42). In other words, they were a worshiping and a praying people. The "breaking of bread" here means more than that they simply ate their meals together, even though I would argue that eating together is a characteristically Christian activity. When I was first planting a church in England, I asked a number of older pastors for advice. One man leaned back in his chair and thought deeply before replying, "Everything goes better with food." It took me a while to work out what he meant by that, but there is a rich biblical theology on sharing meals together. We "ought not to neglect eating together," to slightly misquote Hebrews 10:25! However, in context here, the breaking of bread refers to the fellowship that was shared by the early Christians at their simple communion services.[4] Thus, one

4 Simon J. Kistemaker, *Acts*, New Testament Commentary (Baker, 1990), 111.

of the key descriptors of these believers was that they were devoted to worshiping together.

Now you might respond, "Well, that's not very surprising; surely people expect Christians to worship." I suggest that what people actually expect, however, is for Christians to go to church, that mysterious and rather boring place, where people sit on uncomfortable pews for an hour singing some old-fashioned hymns and listening to a dull and irrelevant talk. What they certainly don't expect is that you go there to worship; that is, that you go to church week after week seeking that your heart would be overwhelmed and your mind freshly dazzled with the profound glory of who God is and what he has done for you in the gospel. For most observers, that would be a truly bizarre thought!

Notice too which aspect of the worship service is prominent in this description: the breaking of bread. It is not that the early church didn't have a high view of preaching. On the contrary, they were devoted to the apostles' doctrine. They loved preaching. But they also loved gathering together for the Lord's Supper. They understood what many Christians have come to appreciate: that celebrating the Lord's Supper focuses our eyes and our hearts on the gospel in a unique and powerful way that preaching alone cannot. It does so because the Lord's Supper is itself a means of grace: It is a gift given to us by the Lord, wherein his Holy Spirit promises to be at work within us. It is spiritual food that strengthens us for our long and weary pilgrimage to heaven. It is a meal to strengthen weak faith. Most people outside the church don't get that: How can a scrap of bread and a sip of wine really make a difference in your life? Doesn't it become merely a boring ritual after a while? Is there some kind of magic power attached to the elements, as Catholicism proclaims? No, not at all! The bread remains bread, and the wine remains wine, but through the power of the Holy Spirit, the Lord's Supper becomes a foretaste of glory, a profound anticipation of the reality of heaven that you can receive without even having to go through a near-death experience. The efficacy of the Lord's Supper doesn't rest on our emotional response to it; it is not a mere memorial in which we remember what Jesus did for us. Rather, the Lord's

Supper works because through these ordinary means God works in us, strengthening our faith and pointing us afresh to Christ and the gospel.

The Lord's Supper also binds us together as a united community of worshipers. Paul tells the Corinthians,

> The cup of blessing that we bless, is it not a participation in the blood of Christ? The bread that we break, is it not a participation in the body of Christ? Because there is one bread, we who are many are one body, for we all partake of the one bread. (1 Cor. 10:16–17)

Notice where the unity that is expressed in the Lord's Supper comes from. It doesn't come from pursuing unity in itself; rather, it comes from our common participation in Christ. As we agree on the gospel and the essential elements of the faith, we are united together more deeply in expressing that faith—as we eat and drink together at the Lord's Table. The Lord's Supper is the family meal for the people of God. And this is why access to the Lord's Supper is limited to those who have publicly professed their faith in Christ and who have committed themselves to a local body of believers.

Worship at Home

So far we've been talking about corporate worship, where we come together to sing God's praises. Yet according to Acts 2, people should also find strange your commitment to informal worship as well. The early church met daily in the temple courts. But they also met in people's own homes (Acts 2:46), apparently for informal services and fellowship. Now I think that in some ways people find it easier to understand our commitment to formal public worship together than to informal worship. People can understand why you might want to go to an aesthetically beautiful church building with a fine music program or an outstanding speaker. They can even understand to some extent your desire to go to church on Sundays, even though none of those things may be present. Perhaps church attendance is just force of habit for you, or a place to make useful social connections. What else is there to do on a rainy Sunday morning, after all? But most people will not understand a commitment to living a life of praise to God that overflows conventional bounds and delights in spending time praising God with others privately as well as publicly.

To meet together every day in the temple courts and also break bread together in their own homes, as the early church did (Acts 2:46), seems like a pretty fanatical schedule to the average non-Christian—and even to many Christians. Every day they were in church, plus they had small groups with whom to pray and study and worship! We have to admit that the early Christians' enthusiasm sometimes seems strange: most of us have had times—sometimes for months or even years—when we have gone to church week after week without ever being moved in a profound and deep way. Perhaps we may begin to wonder whether we have ever really worshiped God with all our being. Do we really have such a deep and insatiable appetite for worship that it surprises those around us? Christians are to be peculiar in their love of worship. That is precisely what happened to the early church: they were carried away in their love and devotion to their Lord, and their desire to be with God's people praising him knew no bounds.

Let me suggest that this is certainly an area where most Christians are not nearly strange enough. Many of us find it much easier to talk to one another about our work, our hobbies, our classes, our sports, or our relationships than we do to talk to one another about our God. When we're in church, we sing God's praises, perhaps, but outside the regular services, our lips are often far more occupied with the praise of other things.

Of course, not all life is lived on the emotionally high plane we see in the first days of the church in Jerusalem. It would be thoroughly exhausting for us if it were.[5] Even in the book of Acts as a whole, we don't see this pattern being maintained. And in our personal lives, there will be

5 C. S. Lewis points out this reality with respect to the initial emotion of falling in love, which is necessarily unsustainable over the long term. He says, "Who could bear to live in that excitement for even five years? What would become of your work, your appetite, your sleep, your friendships?" Lewis, *Mere Christianity* (G. Bles, 1969), 86.

times when we go through seasons of drought, when the times of worship that once thrilled us leave us apathetic and unmoved. This common Christian experience underlines the connection between the Holy Spirit being poured out at Pentecost earlier in the chapter and the outcomes described in this passage. Only the Holy Spirit can stir up our hearts with this kind of passion, and he doesn't always grant us that gift—but we should long for God to give us a greater hunger to praise him!

Committed to Prayer

Similarly, people may expect you as a Christian to pray; what they won't expect is the kind of commitment to prayer that we see in the early church (Acts 2:42). If people know that you are a Christian, they may ask you to say a few words of blessing over the food, or even to lift up a particular need before God for them. As a pastor and seminary professor, I meet people in everyday life who sometimes ask me to "say a prayer" for them. People may expect you to pray before an exam or an operation. But they really won't expect you to be devoted to prayer. If you are, you will seem peculiar.

One thing I have observed in my travels is that wherever you find a good church—a church that seems to be particularly powerful in its worship and preaching, that is especially effective in its ministry to believers and in its outreach to unbelievers—you usually find this common factor: a commitment to prayer. Now there are a variety of different ways in which churches do this; there is no universal formula. Some churches have a large weekly prayer meeting at which a significant portion of the church comes together to pray. Other churches have lots of small group meetings in which prayer is a central part. Both approaches have their strengths and weaknesses, but the key in both cases is that people pray.

I don't know about you, but this is an area that I personally find a real struggle. I need to learn and continually to relearn how to make every area of my life subject to prayer. I need to find people whom I meet with individually on a regular basis and say, "What's God doing in your life that I can praise him for?" and "How can I pray for you today?" It has been a great blessing in some of the churches in which I have served to have people who constantly encourage those around them to pray. We need one another in this area, if we are truly to be devoted to prayer.

A Multiplying Community

The most surprising thing of all about Christians, however, is their power to multiply. I'm not talking about the fact that Christians tend to have larger families than non-Christians, though there are some very good reasons for that. I'm talking about the last verse of the passage we've been examining: "And the Lord added to their number day by day those who were being saved" (Acts 2:47). Nowadays, most people expect churches to grow largely by people moving from another church. It is tempting to think that if we offer a better program, better preaching, and better music than other places of worship around us, perhaps we can snag some more attendees and build a bigger church. It's not necessarily wrong for people to leave one church to go to another. Sometimes there are good reasons to leave a church—because the Bible is not being preached, for example, or the people are not being faithfully shepherded.

Real church growth, though, is not just people moving from other churches, bringing their gifts and talents with them. It can be a wonderful blessing and encouragement when people do that, but real church growth comes as God changes people's unbelieving hearts and brings them into a living relationship with him. No non-Christian expects people to get converted; of course not, because it flies in the face of everything they believe. That is why probably the most powerful testimony anyone can ever see is the changed life and lifestyle of a personal friend who has just become a Christian. When people see someone they know well suddenly becoming devoted to God's word, experiencing the fellowship of God's family, continually talking about how wonderful God is and the answers to prayer that they are receiving, then they too will be overcome with awe.

The difficulty, however, is that we cannot bring about that change in anyone's life by ourselves. It is the Lord who added to the numbers of the early church in Jerusalem, and it will be the Lord who adds to our numbers. Growing the church is not a matter of slick marketing or social psychology. It is not about presentation and appearance; it is about changed hearts and lives. The Lord is the only one who can bring about that kind of new birth and transformation. But surely heart transformation ought to be the focus for our prayers. If we want to have an impact on our community for Jesus Christ, then we should be serious about praying for people in our communities to be converted by the power of the Holy Spirit and be added to our churches. The gospel—not programs or entertainment or a beautiful building—is what will draw people to us.

The One Foundation

Certainly we should desire with all our hearts that people would find our churches to be surprising: surprising in their commitment to the apostles' teaching, to fellowshiping together, to worshiping in formal and informal settings, to praying, and to seeing God convert people in our midst. However, by itself that could be an intimidating and crushing vision. You may be thinking to yourself, "Wow, I fall so short of what a real Christian ought to look like! And our church has such a long way to go as a church to be anything like that church in Jerusalem in Acts 2!" Those are not necessarily bad thoughts to have: Acts 2 does give us a glorious vision of what the church can be, and we should long to be the kind of Christians who would feel right at home there. But in addition to having those thoughts, we need to remember two other vitally important realities.

First, we need to notice that the sovereign God, who poured out his Spirit on the church at Pentecost, has not chosen to make every church to be like that first assembly of believers. He could have done so. All things are equally possible for him. But most of the churches we meet on the pages of the New Testament are deeply broken churches. Galatia was ready to turn their backs on the gospel (Gal. 1:6), Corinth was tolerating immoral behavior (1 Cor. 5:1–2), Thyatira was tolerating a false teacher (Rev. 2:20), and even Ephesus had lost its first love (Rev. 2:4). As we go further in the book of Acts, we start to see problems emerging even in the church in Jerusalem. It is as if God, having shown us a glimpse of the ideal Spirit-empowered church, then shows us the more normal state of the church, which is chaos and disarray.

The same is also true of our lives as individual Christians. None of us has the kind of commitment to the apostles' teaching, to fellowship, to worship, to evangelism, and to prayer that we ought. Indeed, sometimes we had more enthusiasm for these things in the days when we first became believers than we have now, after many years walking with God. The God who could by his Spirit sanctify us immediately has not chosen to do so: he has chosen to leave us very weak and broken people so it may be clear that all the power is his, and his too is all the glory.

That leads us to the second vital thought, flowing out of the first, which I might state like this: I am so glad that I have a glorious Savior who has saved me just as I am and who has committed himself to build his church by his power and not by mine. The first Christians knew themselves to be sinners, profoundly broken people. Among them were some of the very people who had crucified the Lord Jesus. But they also knew themselves to be forgiven sinners who had repented of their sins and received mercy from God for Jesus's sake. They knew that Jesus Christ didn't simply come to earth to model this kind of ideal lifestyle for them—a life devoted to God's word, to fellowship with God's people, to worship, to prayer, to the conversion of men and women. More than a mere example, Jesus lived that wholly devoted life perfectly as a substitute for them. He obeyed the law in their place and in ours. When he was here among us, Jesus reveled in studying and teaching God's word; he poured himself joyfully into fellowshiping with the disciples and other believers. Jesus also delighted to worship his Father and to pray to him in public and in private. And Jesus poured out his life, quite literally, to seek and save the lost (Matt. 1:21). Jesus Christ with his perfect righteousness is his church's only foundation, the foundation on whom we will all have to rest, even on our best days. The gospel is not, "Try hard to be just like the church in Acts 2 and then God will love you"; the gospel is the good news that Christ's righteousness is enough, even for churches and Christians that fall so far short of that Acts 2 fervor. As Jesus himself said, "I will build my church, and the gates of hell shall not prevail against it" (Matt. 16:18).

That promise is, of course, precisely what gave the early church such a powerful drive to worship and to gather regularly to break bread! They knew how much they had been loved by God and how much they had been forgiven through the gospel. That experience of grace is what gave them such a commitment to apostolic doctrine and to rich fellowship together: they knew the reality of their own sins and blindness, and as a result were both devoted to biblical truth and incredibly tolerant and patient with fellow sinners in their tottering first steps toward holiness. That's what gave the early believers in Acts such a commitment to prayer. They knew that they were desperately weak and that whatever strength they had could come only from the Lord, through the work of his Spirit. It is the gospel that picks us up and encourages us when we fall short, and it is the gospel that drives us on to ever greater obedience.

When grace overflows in our lives so that we see more and more clearly who God is and what he has done for us in Jesus Christ, then we too will daily become more "peculiar," more distinct from those around us, more in love with the one who saved us through his blood and who deserves all our worship and praise. And our churches will increasingly resemble the sort of community God intends them to be, in spite of all their warts, for the watching world to see.

6

At the Name of Jesus

Acts 3

THERE ARE MANY different ways to introduce a sermon. Some preachers like to start with a joke or a story from everyday life. Some begin with an attention-grabbing statement or statistic. Others simply plunge right in without any proper introduction at all. Peter certainly begins his first recorded sermon after the day of Pentecost with an attention grabber, but in this case it is not what he says but what he does: he heals a man who has been born lame. The function of this miracle is not simply to help this one man and improve his personal life situation, though it certainly does those things; these miracles have a particular purpose. They are signs.

Acts 2:43 prepares the way for this event when it speaks in a summary way of "many wonders and signs" being done by the apostles. And here we have the first example. As with road signs, miraculous signs are not an end in themselves. The goal of a sign is not to make you say, "What a beautifully crafted sign!" Rather, signs are designed to point away from themselves toward something else. These miraculous signs undergirded and prepared the way for the preaching of the word and pointed people to the truth of the good news about Jesus Christ.

These days it is fashionable to quote the dictum attributed to Francis of Assisi, "Preach the gospel at all times; when necessary, use words."[1] The reality is, of course, that by definition preaching the gospel always includes words. In the book of Acts we regularly see the apostles using words to preach the gospel, as Peter does here. The sign of healing the man is a visual aid that prepares for, supports, and authenticates the proclamation of salvation to be found in the name of Jesus, but it cannot communicate the heart of that gospel. What the sign does in this passage is to point us toward the power, blessing, and authority that reside in the name of Jesus.

The Power of the Name of Jesus

To begin with, the passage shows us the power that there is in the name of Jesus. Luke records the healing in a rather matter-of-fact way: "A man lame from birth was being carried" (Acts 3:2). Clearly, his problem wasn't merely that he had a sprained ankle or something that might get better on its own. Every day people would carry the man to the gate of the temple so that he might eke out a living by begging there. There was an ironic contrast between the loveliness of his surroundings—the Beautiful Gate, a 75-foot-high gate made from Corinthian brass[2]—and the tragedy of a man unable to walk, crippled from birth. The temple gateway was probably a good location for begging, as worshipers entering the temple were more likely than the average person to generously give alms. But sadly this was also probably as close to the temple itself as this man ever got: as someone with a disability, he was likely barred from access to the temple grounds themselves.[3] Only those who were whole were permitted into the presence of God, a requirement that was emblematic of the need for perfect holiness if you were to stand before the Lord. It may have been time for the afternoon sacrifice inside the

1 To be fair to Francis, as far as we know he never actually said that; the earliest known source attributing it to him dates back only to 1991.

2 John R. W. Stott, *The Message of Acts: To the Ends of the Earth*, The Bible Speaks Today (InterVarsity, 1990), 90.

3 Patrick Schreiner, *Acts*, Christian Standard Commentary (Holman Reference, 2021), 153.

temple and the daily prayers that went with that sacrifice, but that was not something that the crippled man could take part in.

Meanwhile, Peter and John are going up to the temple to join in those afternoon prayers (Acts 3:1). They probably did this every afternoon—remember, the early church met together every day in the temple courts (2:46). But on this particular day as they are going into the temple, the lame man calls out to them and asks for money (3:3). Peter stops and instructs the man to look at them—which of course he does, hoping for a substantial gift. What he receives is something far better than silver or even gold. Peter says to him, "In the name of Jesus Christ of Nazareth, rise up and walk!" And he does so, not merely stiffly staggering to his feet but walking and leaping and praising God (3:8). Luke's description explicitly links this man's healing back to the prophecies of the Old Testament, specifically to Isaiah 35, in which the Lord promised a new exodus for his scattered people, bringing them back to Zion, the temple mountain. In response to this new act of deliverance on the Lord's part, the desert would blossom, the blind would see, the deaf would hear, the mute would sing for joy, and, yes, the lame would leap like deer (Isa. 35:5–6). Here in Acts, in fulfillment of this prophecy, when the lame man is healed, he leaps around like a deer and his silent tongue is loosened in praise to God.

But this miracle is not something that Peter and John accomplish in their own power. They don't walk up to the lame man and say, "Rise up and walk!" Rather, they say, "In the name of Jesus Christ of Nazareth, rise up and walk" (Acts 3:6). What is more, when a crowd gathers in awe of this miracle, the first thing Peter does is make clear who has performed it. This man has not been healed by the apostles' own power or godliness; rather, it is by faith in the name of Jesus that this man has been made strong (3:16).

This miracle did not occur because the name of Jesus is some kind of magical incantation, as the seven sons of Sceva discovered to their cost later in the book of Acts (Acts 19:13–16). You can't just say, "In the name of Jesus," and get whatever you want. Rather, the name of Jesus represents the person of Jesus, who is still at work in the world even though he has now ascended into heaven. Perhaps the most surprising aspect of this miracle is Peter's comment to the crowd in verse 12: "Men of Israel, why do you wonder at this?" What Peter is saying is, "What's the big surprise? Are you astonished at someone who has been crippled from birth suddenly walking? This is simply the power of Jesus at work." Remember what Luke wrote in his introduction to the book of Acts. He said, "In the first book, O Theophilus, I have dealt with all that Jesus *began* to do and teach" (Acts 1:1). The rest of the book of Acts is about what Jesus *continued* to do and teach through the early church.

So it shouldn't be a surprise to any of the onlookers at the temple that day to see the power of Jesus still at work. The one who made the blind to see, who healed the crippled, and who raised the dead while he lived here on earth is still active in bringing wholeness into the world. He is turning back the effects of the curse that came with the first Adam's sin. His name has the power to bring about the changes that Isaiah 35 anticipated: an end to Israel's exile and a restoration of this fallen and broken world to a wholeness unknown since mankind was driven out of the garden of Eden (Gen. 3:22–24).

The Identity of the Name

In the Bible the miraculous is never an end in itself. The power of the name serves to illuminate the identity of the name. The miraculous power of Jesus's name is primarily of value insofar as it provides an opportunity for the apostles to preach the gospel about who this Jesus is. So when Peter and John heal this man, they don't shout "Hallelujah! Let's hold healing meetings in the Jerusalem Town Hall for the next seven nights." No, they say, "Now that we've got your attention, let us tell you about Jesus." The apostles were not in the business of healing people; they were in the business of telling people about Jesus. After all, even though this lame man has been dramatically healed, he would still one day get sick and die. Physical healing is a genuine blessing, a foretaste of heaven. But by itself it doesn't address humanity's deepest need for deliverance.

Peter begins his sermon by talking about God. Not just a generic god, but Yahweh, the God of Abraham, Isaac, and Jacob (Acts 3:13). This God, he says, has glorified his servant, Jesus. Again, alert listeners would have picked up the Old Testament reference: in Isaiah 52:13, the Lord says,

> Behold, my servant . . . ;
> he shall be high and lifted up,
> and shall be exalted.

Peter is identifying Jesus as the promised glorified servant of the Lord in Isaiah. But this servant himself shares divine characteristics with the Lord—the servant is "high and lifted up" in Isaiah 52, which mirrors the description of the Lord in Isaiah 6:1, where the prophet saw the Lord sitting on a throne in his temple, "high and lifted up."

Peter further emphasizes the divine attributes of Jesus by calling him "the Holy and Righteous One" (Acts 3:14). In the book of Isaiah, the Lord is repeatedly named "the Holy One" or "the Holy One of Israel" (29 times in all); the Lord is also called the "Righteous One" (Isa. 24:16). Meanwhile, in Isaiah 53:11, the servant is called "the righteous one," providing another link between the Lord, his servant, and Jesus. What is more, Peter calls Jesus "the Author of life" (Acts 3:15). He is the one from whom life flows, as is evidenced by the way in which his name brought life and health into the dead limbs of the crippled man. Who is the source of life? God is. He raised Jesus from the dead (3:15). But Jesus is also the author of life because Jesus is himself God. The miracle performed in Jesus's name attests Jesus's deity.

But this is where the sermon gets tricky for Peter's hearers, for as Peter points out, they failed to recognize Jesus as the Holy and Righteous One. On the contrary they denied him and asked for an unholy, unrighteous one—a murderer—to be released by Pilate in his place (Acts 3:14). Far from seeing Jesus as the Lord and Author of life, they killed him. Yet God has now vindicated and glorified this same Jesus, the Messiah whom they rejected, first by raising him from the dead and now by exalting his name as the means of bringing life and health to this shattered man (Acts 3:16).

Peter then calls his hearers to repent and turn around, placing their trust in the name of Jesus as the promised deliverer appointed by God, the suffering servant whose blood alone could wipe away their sins (Acts 3:19). They must listen to Jesus, for he is the promised "prophet like Moses" about whom Deuteronomy 18:15 spoke (Acts 3:22). If Jesus is truly the "Holy and Righteous One," the "Author of life," then spiritual life, health, and peace are not to be found anywhere else except in his name. The people to whom Peter preaches should look forward to the blessing that is to be found in the name of Jesus, to the time when that name will be exalted above every name (Phil. 2:9–11). There is a day coming when every knee will bow at the name of Jesus and every tongue confess that he is Lord to the glory of God the Father.

Indeed, the healing of the lame man is itself a sign foreshadowing the full restoration of all things as anticipated in Isaiah 35. It is a sign of the ending of the human exile from God's presence caused by our sin. It is a sign of the ending of all sickness, pain, sorrow, and suffering, of the ending even of the last enemy, death itself. When this same Jesus returns to earth in triumph, then indeed God's purpose of blessing for the whole world through the seed of Abraham will finally reach its fruition (Acts 3:25). All nations will find a blessing for themselves in Jesus, beginning in Jerusalem and then spreading, as the book of Acts unfolds, to Judea, Samaria, and to the ends of the earth—even to us (Acts 1:8). As Peter says in Acts 2:21, quoting the prophet Joel, "Everyone who calls upon the name of the Lord shall be saved" (Joel 2:32). That "name of the Lord" is none other than the name of Jesus.

Present-day readers must also choose how they will respond to the reality of this exalted and powerful name of Jesus. For those who may not yet have trusted in Christ, this passage fires a warning shot across your bow. You may not be physically disabled like the lame man, so you might not think you need Jesus. You may not feel any guilt over the crucifixion of Jesus: that was long ago and far away. Perhaps you claim that you wouldn't have been among those who voted for the release of Barabbas the terrorist or that you wouldn't have sided with those who shouted to crucify Jesus.

None of us can escape so easily. We are all spiritually disabled before God: we are as unable to keep God's holy law as the crippled man was to walk. In fact, our situation is far worse: We aren't simply disabled but spiritually dead (Eph. 2:1–3). We sometimes can't tell the difference between good and evil, while at other times we know but don't care. We all vote daily in favor of sin, the same sin that brought death into the world, murdering our own souls. At best we ignore the Lord, who is the source of true spiritual life and health. We repeatedly choose our own worldly wisdom over his wisdom. We love our own evil ways rather than his holy paths.

Isaiah 53 says of the servant,

> He grew up before him like a young plant,
> and like a root out of dry ground;
> he had no form or majesty that we should look at him,
> and no beauty that we should desire him.
> He was despised and rejected by men,
> a man of sorrows and acquainted with grief;
> and as one from whom men hide their faces
> he was despised, and we esteemed him not. (Isa. 53:2–3)

If you are not trusting in the name of Christ for your salvation at this very moment, you are despising and rejecting Jesus; you are regarding his deep suffering on the cross as an utter irrelevance to your life; you are treating him and everything that he stands for as without value. How will you find life if you reject the one who is alone the source of all life? Come to him and receive life in abundance, forgiveness for your sins, and an eternal inheritance that cannot perish, spoil, or fade (1 Pet. 1:4). Jesus is not merely a good teacher, one voice of spiritual wisdom among many: he is God himself in human flesh. The name of Jesus is the only name in which we may find salvation.

Healing and the Christian Life

Christians, too, must respond to the miraculous healing of Acts 3—and to the sermon that was subsequently directed to the watching unbelievers. This event, and Peter's inspired interpretation of it, challenge us to think deeply about the sufferings and disappointments in our own lives. For this passage makes it clear that God has the ability to take suffering away with a snap of his fingers, any time he likes. The God who is the source of life, who in the name of Jesus healed this man's broken body, could heal you or your friends or family members. He could resolve your relationship issues. He could fix any or all of your problems instantaneously. Perhaps you have prayed repeatedly that he would do so. And so far he has chosen not to. You are still "lame," in whatever specific form that disability takes in your experience. Why would a God who has the power to transform your life in this way not choose to use it to deliver you and instead leave you struggling to survive?

The answer some people give is that you just don't have enough faith. If only you had more faith, then God would heal you. But there is no indication in Acts 3 that the man is healed by the strength of his own faith. He is healed by faith in Jesus, that is true; but it is Peter and John's faith rather than his that is prominent here. It is their faith that leads Peter to say, "In the name of Jesus Christ of Nazareth, rise up and walk" (Acts 3:6). Peter doesn't wait to see how much faith the man has; instead, he takes him by his hand and raises him to his feet (3:7). If healing were dependent upon the robustness of the man's faith, then ultimately he would have been healed by himself rather than by the name of Jesus.

So why don't we see more dramatic healings like this today? If God still has the power, which he does, and we still have the need, which we do, why doesn't our heavenly Father act to solve all our problems? The answer to this question points us to the "now and not yet" of our salvation. In the "now," our lives are being conformed to the pattern of our crucified Savior. Having identified Jesus as the exalted servant of Isaiah 52:13, Peter immediately goes on to identify Jesus as the suffering servant of Isaiah 53. He shows that not only Isaiah 53 but "all the prophets" of the Old Testament spoke, each in their own way, of the coming suffering of the Christ (Acts 3:18). Christ's brutal death on the cross was no accident of fate, no failure of his faith; rather, it was the predetermined plan of God to take into himself our sin, our sorrows, and our sicknesses on the cross—all the curse that our sin brings into this broken world (Acts 4:28). Having redeemed us through a broken Messiah, rather than immediately delivering us from all our continuing brokenness, instead he chooses to support and uphold us through our suffering, conforming us in that way to the image of Jesus. As was the case for Daniel's three friends, Shadrach, Meshach, and Abednego, God saves us by walking with us through our suffering rather than ensuring that we bypass painful experiences (Dan. 3; cf. Isa. 43:1–3).

But the healing of the lame man is a sign that it shall not always be like this. Jesus was the crucified Messiah, but now he is the resurrected and exalted Messiah, gloriously seated at the Father's right hand (Acts 3:13–15). He will return from there at the proper time to bring a full end to our exile and to this earth's curse. He will make the desert bloom, and every sickness and disability to disappear, swallowed up in wholeness and joy as promised in Isaiah 35 (Acts 3:20–21).

In the meantime, we may experience seasons of refreshing even now. God is at work in our lives by his Holy Spirit. He is always at work, whether we can see him or not, and he cannot be stopped (Phil. 1:6). We see this in action whenever he brings a sinner to new life in him. Bringing a dead soul to life and replacing a hard heart of stone with a responsive heart of flesh is a far greater miracle than merely healing someone's crippled legs! The Holy Spirit is also at work in our lives to sanctify us, changing us more and more into Christ's likeness. He often does his most powerful transformative work precisely through our sufferings, as well as through our struggles with sin and failure. At times, God frees us from some physical or spiritual difficulty, out of his love and kindness. He says to us, "In the name of Jesus Christ, be whole!" And we are. Our sickness is gone! Our besetting sin is taken away—and like the lame man we leap and rejoice.

At other times, however, God chooses to leave us with our burden of brokenness. He says to us, "I like you better with your disability; I love the beautiful fruit of humility and dependence that it bears, along with the way it increases your love for the gospel." As he said to the apostle Paul, "My grace is sufficient for you" (2 Cor. 12:9). But whether he heals us or leaves us broken, it is always an expression of his love for us as his children. He always says to us, "Look forward to the day when this trouble will be no more, and the promise I made to Abraham long ago will finally find its fruition. Look forward to the day when men and women will come into my kingdom from the north and the south and the east and the west through faith in the name of Christ and will find for themselves a blessing in him. Look forward patiently to the day when Christ himself will return to set all things straight, to wipe away every tear and heal every hurt, to make everything sad become a source of joy, and to be recognized fully as bearing the name that is above every name."

Healing and the Kingdom Mandate

This passage also addresses how we think about the church's broader mission to humanity. Sometimes Christians ask whether churches should get involved in social action. Should we be helping people or simply preaching the gospel? For Peter and John, the two callings went hand in hand: they helped the lame man, and then they preached the gospel. As we said earlier, the miracle was a sign authenticating them as the messengers of Jesus and demonstrating his power.

But beware! Preaching the gospel is what really upsets people. The world doesn't mind us helping people, or even doing miracles if we are able to; it will respect and admire you if you are engaged in ministries that help the blind and the lame, the poor and the broken, so long as you don't mention Jesus. What the world resents, however—and resents very much—is the fact that we feel compelled to talk about Jesus all the time. Why are Peter and John arrested in Acts 4? It is not because they healed the lame man. Nobody had a problem with that. They are arrested because they are proclaiming that Jesus was the one who had healed the lame man (Acts 4:2).

This opposition to the gospel has important application to all of us who are Christians. We are not apostles, and most of us are not preachers. We are not called to go around doing signs and wonders or preaching in the name of Jesus. But we are called to give an answer to those who ask us for a reason for the hope that is in us, as Peter tells us in 1 Peter 3:15. We are each walking miracles. There is no greater miracle than the work of God which takes rebellious sinners, who, whether outwardly righteous or outwardly disgraceful, have set themselves up in their hearts as their own gods, and makes them into obedient and loving children of God. Conversion is an amazing thing, and a changed life can be a powerful testimony to others.

The problem comes if you are willing, like Peter and John, to move beyond talking about the miracle to talking about who Jesus is and the inevitable claims that he makes on the other person's life. Christianity is by its very nature an "offensive" religion. It's not that we must be obnoxious in the way we share our faith—sometimes we are a lot more offensive than we need to be. It is simply the fact that as Christians, we can never be content with people saying, "I'm glad you have found something that works for you." We believe in Jesus not because he "works for us"—indeed, God doesn't "work for us." He doesn't exist to serve us but rather the other way around. We believe in Jesus because he is who he says he is: the way and the truth and the life (John 14:6). Jesus is still the name above every name, whether he solves our problems or chooses to leave us deeply broken.

We cannot tone down that message: Jesus is the source of life, and there is no other way to God apart from him. As Peter himself will say a few verses later on: "There is salvation in no one else, for there is no other name under heaven given among men by which we must be saved" (Acts 4:12). It is this exclusivity in the Christian message that those who are not Christians will never understand or forgive us for. It is this reality that lands Christians in prison time and again: not the miracles, not the doing of good, but the proclaiming, clearly and unequivocally, that only in Jesus Christ is there salvation to be found. That is the way it will be until Christ returns, or until the full number of the martyrs have shed their blood for this testimony, as the book of Revelation puts it (Rev. 6:11).

One final word: the now and not yet of our situation in this world also puts limits on our expectations of how much we can help people. Peter and John could heal this man's lameness, but he would still one day get sick and die. That relativizes all our good deeds for the sake of others. Yes, we can and should help people around us in whatever ways we are able. It is good for churches to be a blessing to their community, especially to those who are broken, to those who are the last, the least, and the lost in society. It is good for us to serve others. But we can help them only so far. Even insofar as we are able to solve their earthly problems, only faith in Christ can solve their deepest problem, which is their exile from the presence of God. Only trust in Christ's death and resurrection can give them an inheritance that transcends the brokenness of this world.

Helping meet people's needs is good. But if we are to help them profoundly, it will require us to speak the gospel to them (using words), and to pray that God himself would lay hold on their hearts and add them to the new Israel he is making through faith in Christ. Then, with their souls made whole in Christ, they will have something truly to leap and sing about, whether or not God chooses to heal their other hurts right now. This is the blessing that God promised to Abraham, the blessing that comes to all families of the earth through faith in his seed, Jesus himself. This is the good news that has come to us and has been entrusted to us for the sake of others, as we look forward together to the day when we will see the glorious things that have been promised in him.

7

Holy Boldness

Acts 4:1–31

IT'S HARD NOT TO LOVE the story of Cinderella, the poor and neglected girl dressed in rags who is suddenly transformed into a gorgeous princess at the wave of the fairy godmother's magic wand. The idea behind the Cinderella story is the basis for many television commercials. They show you the before and after shots of a particular person and try to persuade you that their product is the magic wand that made all the difference. Whether it's getting rid of dandruff, regaining control of your finances, or losing that extra weight, there is no shortage of would-be fairy godmothers out there. The trouble is that the change that these products and people offer is merely superficial. Even if they do rid you of your dandruff, your debt, and your love handles, underneath you will still be the same person you always were. When midnight comes, the coach is recognizable as a pumpkin, and the coachmen are nicely dressed, sweetly perfumed rats. No lasting, foundational change has been brought about.

Profound Change

It is not so with the changes that Jesus brings to a life. Jesus changes people from the inside out, and as a result, the changes that he brings are real, substantial, and lasting. In the last chapter, we saw the dramatic change that the power of Jesus brought into the life of the crippled man. From birth, he had been unable to walk, and because he was physically less than perfect, he was excluded from the temple where the presence of God dwelt. Now the man could not only walk but run and jump and leap to the praise of God (Acts 3:8). Perhaps even more astounding than the change in the crippled man is the change that has been brought about in the disciples. In the space of a few weeks, they went from being a group of terrified individuals huddled away in an upper room for fear of the authorities (John 20:19) to men who walked the streets of Jerusalem and stood in front of the Jewish authorities proclaiming the message of Jesus Christ boldly to anyone and everyone who would listen. Boldness is a key theme in Acts 4 (see vv. 13, 29, 31). Peter in particular had been changed from a coward who denied that he even knew Jesus when he was confronted in the high priest's house on the night before Jesus's crucifixion (Luke 22:54–60) to a courageous witness to the exclusive and unique power of Jesus as the messianic Son of God, the only source of life, health, and peace in this world. This was a miracle every bit as remarkable and as undeniable as the healing of the crippled man.

What gave the apostles their boldness in speaking such an unpopular message? Acts 4 addresses the aftermath of the healing of the crippled man. It shows us Peter and John being arrested by the Jewish authorities and put on trial for their actions—at the same time that many other people were coming to believe in Christ as they saw the lame man healed and heard Peter's preaching. This chapter identifies several sources for the apostles' powerful boldness, sources that challenge our general reluctance and unwillingness to speak out for Christ—especially if we think that people might be offended or angry with us for what we say. This chapter also encourages each of us to find a fresh boldness in speaking for Jesus.

Personal Acquaintance with Jesus

In the first instance, the apostles' boldness comes from their personal experience of Jesus Christ. They may be "uneducated, common men," but they have been with Jesus (Acts 4:13). Even the apostles' enemies recognize that time with Jesus was the source of their confidence.

We have to be a little careful about the description of the disciples as uneducated and untrained men (4:13). People sometimes imagine that this statement means that the apostles had never received any kind of formal education. That is extremely unlikely. Peter and Andrew had been fishermen, as had John, running their own small family businesses. Matthew was a tax collector, and he presumably would have been well versed in financial matters. Had the apostles been totally uneducated, they would not have been able to write much of the New Testament.

No, the point is rather that they had not been through a formal program of theological education, such as the scribes and Pharisees had.[1] Their confidence came not from years of reading learned theological treatises in seminary but from time spent with Jesus. This is a tremendously important truth to understand. Some may have spent a fair amount of time reading theological books, while others haven't, and there is application here for those in both categories. For those of us who have spent time in theological training, there is a real danger that when we speak to others about Jesus, we make things too complicated. My wife is a much better evangelist than I am because she has an ability to cut right through the peripheral questions and get down to the heart of the matter: Who is Jesus? When Jehovah's Witnesses come to the door, it is easy for me to get sidetracked by rabbit trails and therefore to miss the central message we have been given: Jesus Christ—crucified, raised, powerful, the only way of salvation, as we see from Peter's messages in Acts. Some of us need to be reminded that people are not converted ultimately by intellectual arguments but rather as the Holy Spirit gives them new birth and opens up their eyes to who Jesus is.

On the other hand, there is also an application here for those who haven't had any theological training. Perhaps you are tempted to let

1 David G. Peterson, *The Acts of the Apostles*, Pillar New Testament Commentary (Eerdmans; Apollos, 2009), 193.

your lack of knowledge prevent you from speaking up for Jesus. Don't let that absence of training worry you; go ahead and tell people what you do know about Jesus. Again, don't get sidetracked by secondary issues; focus on the central message of the gospel, which is simple. If you want, you can start from the miracle of your own new life in Christ: You can testify to what God has done for you, a sinner, and then move on from there to speak about the objective reality of who Jesus is and his claims on the other person's life. You don't need to have a dramatic personal story for your Christian life to be a miracle; we were all once dead in our sins, and if God had left us to ourselves, we would all still be there. The fact that God has made you his and holds you safely in his hand, and that he has given you a hope and a glorious inheritance in Christ—all this is dramatic enough!

But don't wear your theological ignorance like a badge of pride. Remember that even though the disciples hadn't been formally schooled, they had been with Jesus. They had devoted themselves for three long years to being with him, listening to his teaching, watching him at work, studying him, and learning at his feet. Even though we can't physically go and travel around with Jesus, we can still sit at his feet as we read the Scriptures and study them and as we help one another apply these truths into our hearts and lives. The book of Proverbs tells us that even though God's wisdom is a gift from him, it comes as we search for it like gold or silver, as we immerse ourselves in its pursuit—just as those first disciples immersed themselves in the apostles' teaching (Prov. 2; Acts 2:42). This is how we can be with Jesus, even today. And one mark of that "being with Jesus" ought to be our boldness to declare that same truth to others around us.

Recognizing God's Sovereignty over Creation

The next source of the apostles' boldness comes from their recognition of the sovereignty of God. The apostles remind themselves who is running the world in which they live, and they draw confidence from that knowledge. The idea of God's sovereignty is a doctrine that people sometimes get tied up in knots over, but it is actually practical in its application. God is sovereign over all creation because he made the heavens, the earth, the sea, and everything in them (Acts 4:24).

There's nothing quite like that fact for putting everything else in creation into its proper perspective. If God created everything and everyone in the world, then he created you, with your specific combination of strengths and weaknesses, gifts and sins. Thus, when Moses wanted to use his weakness as a public speaker to evade God's call on him to bring the children of Israel out of Egypt, the Lord said to him, "Who has made man's mouth? Who makes him mute, or deaf, or seeing, or blind? Is it not I, the LORD? Now therefore go, and I will be with your mouth and teach you what you shall speak" (Ex. 4:11–12). God basically says, "I made you the way that you are, with your particular combination of personality and family history, and I put you in these circumstances, so you can look to me to help you and teach you what to say." God is sovereign over all creation, and that should give us boldness to step out in faith and seize the opportunities that he brings to us to speak for him.

If God is sovereign over all creation, he is also the one who must set the agenda for our lives. He is our ultimate King, and we must submit to him. Peter and John recognize this truth in their response to the Jewish leaders: "Whether it is right in the sight of God to listen to you rather than to God, you must judge, for we cannot but speak of what we have seen and heard" (Acts 4:19–20). In other words, they recognize a higher authority than the political and religious leaders of their day. And the same must be true of us. We believe what we believe about God and we do what we do as Christians because God has spoken in his word, and we must obey him—and not because the politicians or the culture or even the church tell us what to do.

There is a delicate balance in this. On the one hand, the government is given a legitimate authority over us, as is the leadership of the church (Rom. 13). The Christian life leaves no place for anarchism or for a radical individualism that rejects all forms of authority. And yet all authorities in this world are subordinate to God and cannot bind our consciences against his word. That means that politicians have a right to make laws about all kinds of issues that are not directly addressed in the Scriptures. Christianity holds no official view of speed limits or of tax policies or even of whether a country should have socialized medicine. Christians can have a variety of views on these subjects as they try to work out how to apply various biblical principles wisely in their own contexts. They are responsible to vote according to their views and then to submit to whatever the ruling authority decides. Yet if the government seeks to force you as a medical professional to perform an abortion, you have to obey God rather than men. There are some things that we cannot in good conscience accede to because the word of God clearly tells us we may not. If we understand that truth, it will give us a holy boldness to stand out from the society around us.

The leaders of the church have a legitimate authority over us too—and yet if they overstep the proper bounds of that authority and seek to bind our consciences contrary to the word of God, we have to draw a line and say, "I can't do that." I had such an experience as a much younger man applying to be a candidate for the ministry of the Church of Scotland. This was a dream that I had been working toward for many years, but in the interview, it emerged that my conservative view on the ordination of women was not acceptable to them. They were perfectly within their rights to turn me down; it is appropriate that ministers in a denomination match up to the theological views of that denomination. What they were not at liberty to do was to say, as one minister said to me, "Well, the church has made up its mind on that subject. You just have to accept that." Nonsense! If the Bible teaches a given truth, I need to believe it and proclaim it, even if every branch of the church denies it. God is my sovereign, and I have to obey him, even if that means leaving a denomination I have been part of for many years. Such an attitude will give us all a humble yet holy boldness in standing for the truth in our churches.

Peter and John's Message

It is all very well to be bold, empowered by the Holy Spirit, but if we're going to speak boldly for God we'd better be sure that we have the message straight. Boldly spoken nonsense won't help anyone. Peter and John's message is really very simple, even though it was offensive to the prevailing religious leadership, both then and now. Jesus died on the cross, was raised from the dead, is now exercising a powerful ministry here on earth, and is the exclusive means of salvation (Acts 4:10–12). Here we see once again a theme that is absolutely unique about Christianity. The message of every other religion stresses the life and teaching of its founder. But Christianity revolves around the death and resurrection of its founder. I remember once talking to a man who was a follower of the Baha'i faith; he told me how much his religion sincerely respects the teaching of Jesus Christ. That's all very well, but the essential message of the early church is not the teaching of Jesus but the death and resurrection of Jesus.

Christianity is an exclusive religion; Peter says that "there is no other name given among men by which we must be saved" (Acts 4:12). There are other religions that have moral teachings that are in some ways very similar to those of Jesus, so if salvation were about getting your morality straight, there would potentially be many ways to approach God. But no other religion under heaven proclaims the death and resurrection of Jesus as our only hope—that it is not Jesus's teaching that saves us but his sacrificial death and his triumphal resurrection. In his righteousness he kept the law spotlessly in our place, his sacrificial death with all our sins laid on him paid the debt that we owed to the sovereign God of the universe, and his resurrection demonstrated the fact that God accepted his sacrifice in our place as full payment for our sins. This is precisely the element that offends people in our presentation of the gospel: the centrality of the cross as our unique means of salvation. People are quite happy for us to teach ethical principles, to tell children how they should live, and to encourage them to follow the Golden Rule. What people really don't want to hear is that all their best moral efforts are worthless and filthy in God's sight (Isa. 64:6) and that salvation comes only when we place our trust in the death and resurrection of Jesus. They especially don't want to hear that there is, and can be, no other way to be saved.

Recognizing God's Sovereignty over the Nations

But there is one more aspect to the apostles' boldness: they understood that God is not only sovereign over creation and over our circumstances but sovereign over all the forces that oppose him. That's the point of the quotation of Psalm 2 in Acts 4:25–26. The ancient psalm predicted that the powers that be would range themselves against the Lord and his Christ (or "anointed one"). The apostles recognized the fulfillment of that prophecy in the conspiracy of Herod and Pontius Pilate—the kings and rulers—with the Gentiles, the nations of Psalm 2. What is even more shocking, though, is that now "the peoples of Israel" (Acts 4:27) have joined together with the rebellious nations of Psalm 2. God's own people have turned against him.

But the point of the quotation from Psalm 2 is not simply to remind us that God has shown us ahead of time the way life will be for his followers and that in this world we should therefore anticipate much tribulation. No, the psalm also goes on to declare God's amusement at all their petty posturing (Ps. 2:4). When he is ready, he will sweep it aside and install his chosen King on Mount Zion (2:6). Quoting Psalm 118:22, Peter declares, "This Jesus is the stone that was rejected by you, the builders, which has become the cornerstone" (Acts 4:11). God is utterly sovereign even over those who oppose him.

This fact was graphically demonstrated in the Old Testament in the story of Joseph (Gen. 37–50). Everything apparently went wrong for Joseph as a result of his brothers' envy. He was sold into slavery in Egypt, where he ended up languishing in prison for a crime he didn't commit. Then he was forgotten by the ones he helped. And yet when he finally met up with his brothers, he said, "You meant evil against me, but God meant it for good" (Gen. 50:20). It's as if he were saying, "You thought you were going to get even with me, breaking every law in God's book in the process, but God was sovereign even over your sinful intentions in such a way as to bring about his own good purposes through your evil purposes."

This same truth was graphically demonstrated to the apostles in the death of Jesus. This conspiracy of evildoers followed their own evil desires when they crucified Jesus; yet at the same time they did only what God's power and will had decided beforehand would occur (Acts 4:28). Do you see how this brings us boldness in the face of opposition? What can people do to us after all? There is nothing they can do to us more than what God decides to permit in his sovereignty and fatherly care.

A story is told of the early church father John Chrysostom, who was on trial for his life at the royal court.[2] The empress said to him, "We will banish you!" to which Chrysostom replied, "You cannot banish me, for the whole world is my Father's home."

"Well then, we will execute you," said the empress.

"You can't. My life is hid with Christ."

"We will dispossess you of your estate."

"You cannot. I haven't got any. All my treasure is in heaven."

"Well then," said the empress finally, "We will put you into solitary confinement."

To which Chrysostom replied, "You cannot; for I have a divine Friend from whom you can never separate me. I defy you. There is nothing you can do to hurt me!"

Children of the living God, coheirs with the risen Christ, we have nothing to fear from men and women whose very rage against us is controlled by the power of God.

Do you see how comforting this truth of God's sovereignty over evil is for us? Some of you readers may be deeply wounded by something profoundly evil that happened to you. Perhaps it was abuse, either physical or sexual, from someone you trusted. Or perhaps you have been betrayed by an unfaithful friend or employer. Nothing can undo the evil that you have suffered or make it right. You can't make it go away or pretend that it didn't happen. But can you see that God is sovereign over this evil too, just as he was over the crucifixion of his own Son? Nothing more evil than the crucifixion has ever happened in the history of the world: How can we not weep over the tragic picture of a perfect human being, cruelly abused, brutally tortured, and then executed in the most foul manner possible? Yet this unspeakable crime was the

2 There is some debate about the exact circumstances and details of precisely what Chrysostom said and under what circumstances he said it, but the thoughts seem to be genuinely his. For a well-documented discussion, see Anonymous, "Chrysostom's Invincibility before the Byzantine Empress," Pioneer Library, November 12, 2017, https://olddeadguys.com.

Father's perfect will, planned long ago in order to bring redemption to a world of sinners. If the sovereign God can bring such good out of such wickedness, he can surely bring something good out of your suffering. The scriptural picture of God's sovereignty can also encourage us when we are fearful of the future, afraid of what may happen to us. Even if the very worst that we can imagine comes to pass, Peter reminds us that the sovereign God who loves us and gave himself for us rules over those circumstances. That can give us boldness to speak for him, even when we are uncertain of the reception that our words will receive.

Filled with the Holy Spirit

There is another crucial element to the apostles' boldness: after they pray, the place where they are meeting is shaken, and they are all filled with the Holy Spirit and speak the word of God boldly (Acts 4:31). It is not just Peter and John who are filled with the Holy Spirit and speak boldly; they are all filled with the Holy Spirit. There is a key link in the book of Acts between being filled with the Holy Spirit and speaking out boldly about Jesus Christ. We saw it already in 2:4: "And they were all filled with the Holy Spirit and began to speak in other tongues as the Spirit gave them utterance." This link is also present in the passage we've been examining in this chapter, notably in Acts 4:8 and 4:31. In Acts 9:17 Paul is filled with the Holy Spirit, and right afterward we see him preaching with power (9:20). Similarly, in Acts 13:9 the result of Paul's being filled with the Holy Spirit is a powerful speech against Elymas. Obviously, boldness isn't the only result of Christians being filled with the Spirit. An abundance of the fruits of the Spirit will also follow: love, joy, peace, and so on. But boldness is a key result. When men and women are full of the Holy Spirit, they speak the word of God boldly. That means that if we want to see the word of God going out from us in power, we need to be praying that God will fill us with his Holy Spirit so that we may speak with boldness and authority the message about Jesus Christ that has been committed to us.

Of course, the reality for most of us is that we are not nearly as bold as we should be in speaking about Jesus. Many of us turn into pumpkins every time an opportunity to share the gospel arises, instead of speaking with great boldness and clarity as the Holy Spirit gives us the words to say. This is why God's utter sovereignty in salvation should be a great comfort to all of us. God is not stymied by our slowness to speak for him. The good shepherd will bring in all his sheep, and not one of them will be lost because of something we failed to say or said imperfectly. The words that really count are the ones that Jesus said for us: "My God, my God, why have you forsaken me?" (Matt. 27:46) and "Father, into your hands I commit my spirit!" (Luke 23:46). His obedience, not ours, is what delivers us from our sins.

Yet at the same time, Jesus calls, commissions, and empowers us to speak that good news for him with great boldness. You may end up seeing people converted by your words; you may end up in jail. There are no guarantees with God, except for these: that God has installed his crucified and exalted anointed one, Jesus Christ, as King over all nations, and that on the last day, all those who are his will enter into glory—not one of his people will be missing.

8

Don't Get Caught Dead in Church

Acts 4:32–5:16

THE BIBLE IS BOTH an exciting and a disturbing book.

On the one hand, it is a book that is filled with exciting accounts of God's grace, mercy, and healing power. We read of the exodus from Egypt, of the walls of Jericho falling down, of David's victory over the giant Goliath, of Daniel triumphing in the lion's den. We read of the power of the Holy Spirit healing a crippled man at the Beautiful Gate of the temple just a couple of chapters earlier in the book of Acts. This is all wonderful, exciting stuff.

But then there are the other stories—what we might designate the darker side of the Bible. There is a flood that exterminates all humanity with the exception of one family (Gen. 6–9). There is the fire from heaven that incinerates the entire towns of Sodom and Gomorrah (Gen. 19). There is the slaughter of many of the indigenous inhabitants of Canaan in the time of Joshua. There is the stoning of Achan and his whole family merely for stealing a few objects from the spoils of Jericho (Josh. 7). These stories are not so wonderful and exciting. They seem dark and disturbing. What do they say about the character of a God who would do such things—and about the people who would follow such a God?

Such a story faces us in Acts 5. Consider what happens here: We have a man and a woman who make an extremely generous donation to the church at considerable personal cost. There is then a minor miscommunication about whether or not their gift represents the whole of the proceeds from the sale of their property. The next thing you know they are both dead, struck down by the hand of God. That's a pretty disturbing picture. Yet if we are going to understand, love, and serve the God of the Bible, we are going to have to come to grips with stories like these.

Let me suggest to you three things we see very clearly in this passage: first, sin is serious business; second, Satan is a seductive adversary; and third, the Holy Spirit still triumphs and adds people to the church.

Sin Is Serious

To begin with, we need to see that sin is serious. I've read many internet discussions of these difficult passages in the Bible, and one thing that is immediately obvious is the difficulty that many people have in comprehending the true weightiness of sin. We find it hard to accept that sin is deadly, even though the Bible explicitly tells us this truth. In Romans 6:23 we are told that the wages of sin is death. What sin deserves—all sin and every sin, sins of omission as well as commission, from the smallest to the greatest infraction of God's holiness—is perpetual separation from the God from whom all life flows. Nonetheless we have a hard time believing that that estimation of sin is really true and right.

The difficulty we have in accepting God's opinion of sin is not new, of course. Back in the garden of Eden, God said to Adam, "Of the tree of the knowledge of good and evil you shall not eat, for in the day that you eat of it, you shall surely die" (Gen. 2:17). But Adam and Eve believed the serpent rather than God when the serpent said, "You will not surely die" (Gen. 3:4). A more liberal approach to sin seemed much more reasonable—why would such a small action lead to death? Yet the consequence of that decision to trust the serpent rather than God was the entry of death for all people into the world. In the same way, God said to his people at Jericho, in effect, "Don't take anything from the spoils of war, for I am the one who wins the victory for you" (see Josh. 6:16–18). But Achan saw some desirable items among the spoils there: a Babylonian robe, some silver, a wedge of gold (Josh. 7:21). It seemed a waste simply to destroy these beautiful things! Surely no one would miss them. And so, while no one was looking, he took them and buried them under his tent. The result was death for himself and his family (Josh. 7:25).

In the same way, Ananias and Sapphira sell a piece of land (Acts 5:1). They wanted to be just like Barnabas, who has sold a field and brought all the proceeds to the apostles for their ministry to the poor (4:36–37). More precisely, Ananias and Sapphira want to be *thought to be* just like Barnabas, without it having to cost them everything they have acquired.

There was no rule in the church that said you had to sell your property, or that if you did, you had to bring all the money to the apostles. Ananias and Sapphira could have gone to the apostles and said, "Here's 10 percent of the proceeds of our field. Use it as you think best." That would have been good—but it wouldn't have been nearly as impressive as what Barnabas had done.

And impressing people is the name of the game for Ananias and Sapphira. They want to give people the impression that they are giving everything to God, while at the same time keeping a little in reserve for themselves. This is their sin. They want to use God as a means to achieve their real goal, which is pleasing the idol of respect and public honor. It seems to them to be only a very small sin, a tiny lie, yet underlying it is a breach of the first commandment. There, God said, "I am the Lord your God who brought you out of the land of Egypt. . . . You shall have no other gods before me" (Ex. 20:2–3). Ultimately that "small" sin—putting their own glory ahead of God—costs them their very lives. Sin is serious business because our God is an awesome, holy God—the same God who revealed himself to Moses in fiery glory at Mount Sinai (see Ex. 19).

Putting it like that helps us see why sin is so serious. We typically think of "sin" in terms of various specific sins: particular outward instances of bad behavior, acts that we then classify into sizes—small, medium, and large. Murder, adultery, and theft would be large sins; outbursts of rage, internet pornography, and cheating on your taxes might be medium-size sins; holding a grudge, everyday lust, and coveting your friend's car are small sins. Of course, these categories are flexible: the sins of others are more likely to rate as medium or large sins, while our own sins are easily classified as small. The devil on our shoulder (which is actually just our flesh), says, "*That* kind of sexual immorality is no big deal—and anyway, we're going to get married. We can be proud and self-centered because we're busy doing important things for God. How unreasonable it would be to expect someone like me to be humble and thoughtful about the needs and desires of those right around me!"

But behind each and every individual sin—whether small, medium, or large—there is a heart attitude from which it flows. Every time we sin, we are putting something else ahead of God's glory. It may be our comfort or our sense of self-importance or our pleasure or our desire for a temporary escape from reality, but there is something that our hearts are valuing at that moment more than the glory of God or obedience to him. That rebellious attitude is what makes each individual sin, however "small," serious in God's sight. It is an act of cosmic treason against our Creator, in which we choose to believe his mortal enemy, Satan, instead of trusting his word. Ironically, like Ananias and Sapphira, we can even turn something that looks like an act of tremendous self-sacrifice and service to God into an opportunity to make others think more positively of us than is really true. Whenever we allow others to have a better image of us than we deserve, we perpetrate a lie and sin not just against them but against God! Such sin has serious consequences.

The deceptiveness of our hearts raises the question, of course, as to how we know when our "good" acts are actually all about us, and thus really acts of cosmic treason. In one sense, of course, all our actions, even our very best ones, are tainted with the poison of self-love. Our motives are always at least somewhat mixed. But it often becomes particularly evident what is driving us when our goals are frustrated. If I am primarily focused on serving God and things don't work out, then I may be disappointed, but I won't be devastated. God is sovereign over that failure too, and he gets to decide how things turn out. But if my eyes are fixed on my idols and I fail, then my idol will curse me and make me miserable, angry, anxious, and depressed. When you counsel people and they don't listen or you preach and no one responds or you do something exceptionally kind for your spouse or your family and they don't even notice—that is when your motivation is revealed. If your goal is pleasing your idols, you will not merely be disappointed but devastated in these situations. You may respond with anger or a fit of sulking, either toward God or those people whom you think got in the way of your plans. You may sink into depression or despair, which is sometimes another form of anger. Your response to your good deeds being ignored exposes your heart.

Satan Is a Seductive Adversary

Satan's role in this story is unmasked by Peter in Acts 5:3. He seduced Ananias and Sapphira to believe that they could sin and not suffer the consequences. He told them that they could lie to God and to man and get away with it. But Satan himself is a liar. He said to Adam and Eve, "You will not surely die. . . . You will be like God" (Gen. 3:4–5). Not only did they in fact die, but they also had the devastating experience of seeing the first death in the world when their oldest son, Cain, murdered his brother (Gen. 4:8). Think of how painful it must have been for Adam and Eve as they saw with their own eyes the consequences of their actions. Far from making them like God, as Satan had promised, their sin resulted in their separation from God as they were driven out of the garden (Gen. 3:24).

Ultimately in Scripture Satan has only three strategies that he uses against God's kingdom: persecution, seduction, and deception. He is a roaring lion who goes about seeking whom he may devour (1 Pet. 5:8). He is drunk with the blood of the martyrs (Rev. 17:6). We saw that aspect of his activity in the previous chapter, as the apostles began to face threats, imprisonment, and the prospect of death for the sake of the name of Jesus (Acts 4:18), threats that will rapidly escalate into actual violence in the chapters ahead. He is also the seductive serpent who insinuated himself into the garden, lisping "Did God actually say . . . ?" (Gen. 3:1), persuading Adam and Eve to view the forbidden fruit with the wisdom of the flesh, not the wisdom of the Spirit. Satan has dressed himself up as an angel of light, seeking, if it were possible, to deceive even the elect (2 Cor. 11:14; Matt. 24:24). He raises up false teachers inside and outside the church, blinding the eyes of many. That aspect of Satan's operations is also visible later on in the book of Acts.

Here in Acts 5, Satan seduces Ananias and Sapphira. He says to them, in essence, "You shall not surely die! No one will uncover your deception. Everyone will think highly of you, the church will benefit from your generous donation, and you will still be able to keep some of the money for yourselves." Satan seduces them—and they die.

How are we similarly being seduced by Satan? Whenever we sin, it is because we are drawn into believing some lie about God, about ourselves, or about where to find true meaning and value in life. For example, coveting is based on the lie that if only I had the object that I covet—my neighbor's wife, his car, his muscles, his athletic abilities, his ability to make people laugh—then my life would be more meaningful and enjoyable than it currently is. Instead of rooting my value as a person in God's love for me in Christ, I'm believing that my value is rooted in something else. Whether that sin of coveting works its way out into actually stealing or destroying what belongs to my neighbor, or whether it simply remains stuffed inside my heart as a jealous attitude, I am sinning against God by believing Satan's lie instead of my Creator's truth. The result is not a life that is filled with more meaning and joy, as Satan suggests, but a life that is filled with more anguish and sorrow, more anger and worry, more broken relationships and frustration. Satan's lies always lead to some form of death, not to life in all its fullness.

The Spirit Keeps Advancing the Kingdom

For Ananias and Sapphira, believing Satan's lies quite literally leads to their deaths. As a result, we're probably not too surprised to read in Acts 5:11 that great fear seizes the whole church and all who hear of these events. That certainly makes sense. We're not surprised to see that the line between the world and the church becomes more distinct as a result, and that those who are not yet believers begin keeping a safe distance from these dangerous disciples.

But perhaps we are a little surprised to read in Acts 5:14 that, in spite of the death of Ananias and Sapphira, more and more men and women believe in the Lord and are added to the church. We don't tend to have too much confidence in the evangelistic potential of divine judgment. We tend to think that church discipline—the process of publicly declaring to people the consequences of their serious, unrepentant sin—will probably put a crimp on our outreach. It is not so in the case of the early church because the Holy Spirit is at work. It is the Lord who is adding to their number (Acts 5:14), not a carefully crafted marketing strategy of telling people that they can love God and live however they like. Surprise! Being biblical turns out to be the best marketing strategy of all, if we are really seeking for God to add disciples to our number, not simply to see a large crowd of people assembled.

But this passage still leaves us with enormous questions. If all sin is really that serious a business, how is any of us left alive? Why doesn't every church need a burial committee to complement the work of the missions committee? If one sin is all it takes for me to deserve a cosmic coronary, why am I still standing here? You would think that if a single act of faulty, half-hearted worship aimed at glorifying ourselves and not God deserves death, then none of us would be left alive at the end of a typical worship service, in which our minds have wandered in a million directions. We may belt out the hymn "I Surrender All," but in our hearts what we are really saying is, "I Surrender Some." We are often far more concerned with what people think of our displays of religiosity than whether the acts we put on display are genuinely pleasing in God's sight. If Ananias and Sapphira deserved to die, so too do you and I.

Signs and Wonders

The answer to those questions gets us to the meaning of the various signs and wonders, both positive and negative, that we see in the book of Acts—and elsewhere in the Bible. Why do some people get dramatically healed by God while others get dramatically killed? Neither of these is God's normal way of dealing with his people during the vast majority of the history of the world. Most sick people in Israel were not healed, and most sinners were not struck down. On the contrary, these miraculous sign-acts—both positive and negative—are concentrated at times of God's special intervention in the world. God didn't normally part the sea in front of people, but he did so at the exodus so that the Egyptians (and the Israelites) would know who delivered the people of Israel from their bondage (see Ex. 14–15). The Israelites were not normally called upon to wipe out their enemies, but the practice of holy war is particularly associated with the conquest of the land in the time of Joshua. These dramatic signs occurred at special times and places in the history of redemption as foreshadowings of the fullness of the kingdom of God.

Given this pattern it is not surprising that we find so many signs and wonders in the Gospels and in the book of Acts. When Jesus Christ came to the earth, the heart of his message was the coming of God's kingdom, a kingdom that brings both life and death—life to those who submit to the coming King and death and destruction to those who oppose the arrival of the Lord's anointed (Matt. 25:31–46). With the coming of Christ, the kingdom of God has indeed arrived on earth, but it is not yet here in its fullness. The kingdoms of this world have not yet become the kingdom of our God and of his Christ (Rev. 11:15). The fullness of the kingdom of God awaits the second coming of Jesus, when every knee will bow before him and every tongue confess his name (Rom. 14:11). Yet in the book of Acts, we start to see the gospel going to the nations; we start to see people from north and south and east and west submitting to the lordship of Christ. The kingdom of God is on the move, and the dramatic signs are foreshadowings of the future. They are exciting trailers for the great "movie" to come.

In other words, the healings of the lame man and of many other sick people in the book of Acts are not a pattern we should expect to see commonly repeated in our own experience. Rather, these healings are a foretaste of the day when the curse on all creation will finally be lifted. On that last day Satan's power will definitively be destroyed, and on that day all the lame will leap for joy, and all the blind will see (Isa. 35:5–6). But in the death of Ananias and Sapphira we get a glimpse ahead of time of the other side of the coin. The return of the Lord Jesus means final judgment for unrepentant sinners, as well as final healing for the cosmos. It means death to all those who are found guilty before the heavenly tribunal, no matter how small their sin may be in their eyes and ours. Ananias and Sapphira simply received their judgment ahead of time, while for others, by God's grace, there is more time left for repentance (2 Pet. 3:7–9). If their hearts are not changed, however, certain death still awaits them in the future. The wages of death must be paid in one way or another for each and every sin.

So the death of Ananias and Sapphira should certainly prevent any complacency with regard to sin. Your sin may not kill you instantly, as theirs did; but any sin, even the least of sins, contains a poison that condemns you not just to earthly death but to eternal torment. There is no antidote for the death that sin brings other than the one that God has provided in Jesus Christ. Sin is serious business, even when it doesn't kill our bodies instantaneously. When we sin we are declaring war on our Creator. And Christ is the only one who can defeat and destroy our sin.

We are called on to take sin seriously, in ourselves and others. If we love people, we cannot let them trifle with something as deadly as sin. That's why we have to be committed to church discipline. If individual members of the church sin seriously and are unrepentant over a period of time, even after we have met with them and sought to show them from Scripture why what they are doing is wrong, we can't just ignore their ongoing rebellion. Rather, we are called to excommunicate them—to declare them publicly outside the bounds of God's kingdom. We need to place in front of people's eyes how serious their sin is. That doesn't mean that we are called to be the thought police, pursuing everyone for every real or imagined transgression. Nor does it mean that if we have to excommunicate someone we should necessarily shun them or ban them from coming to church. On the contrary, we are to treat them like unbelievers (Matt. 18:17),[1] which means that we should desire to speak to them about the gospel as their only hope in life and death. What better place is there for them to hear the message of the only remedy for their sin than in the church? We can't simply conduct business as usual with unrepentant sinners who claim to be Christians; we can't act without reference to their sin. We can't pretend that there is nothing wrong.

What is more, we are also called to take sin seriously in ourselves. Don't trifle with something as deadly as sin! Fear it and flee from it as you would from a deadly snake. When we lived in Africa, my wife was once talking to her cousin and his family when a cobra appeared. Her cousin immediately went to get his camera and started taking pictures of the snake as it gradually approached the kids. All the while, Barb was saying, "Steve . . . Steve . . . isn't it about time you did something about the snake?" He did finally deal with the snake, but it probably would have been wiser not to wait so long. That is certainly true in our dealings with the cosmic serpent, Satan. He is often able to reassure us that our sin isn't serious, that there is no rush to deal with it, that we can continue to cuddle it close to us without any harm done. Don't believe his seductive words. Flee from him as soon as you hear his hiss.

The Sole Remedy for Sin

If sin is indeed so deadly and at the same time is so all-pervasive in our hearts, how shall any of us sinners actually survive life in this sin-cursed world? We have all drunk deeply of the deadly poison, and it regularly erupts into one manifestation of sin or another. You don't have to pursue sin or treat it lightly to find it snuggled up in your heart, even at the very moment while you are trying to worship and serve God. We all have deeply depraved hearts that provide an easy access point for Satan and his seductions. The answer to our desperate need

1 This is a complex passage, and not all commentators agree on its significance. For a good treatment, see John Nolland, *The Gospel of Matthew*, New International Greek Testament Commentary (Eerdmans; Paternoster, 2005), 747.

is the gospel. Our hope of heaven rests precisely in the fact that God takes sin seriously—so seriously that he was not willing to ignore it in us and pretend that it wasn't a problem. Instead, if you are a Christian, God the Father has already meted out the full penalty for your sin, which is death. Instead of pouring it out on you, as you deserve, he has poured it out on Jesus Christ in your place. He became sin for us, being treated by the Father as if he had committed every single one of our sins (2 Cor. 5:21). Jesus Christ was struck down for my transgressions. He was abandoned for my faithless, wandering heart. He was buried for my wrongdoing. His death paid the wages that my sins had earned.

What is more, he lived the life of perfect obedience that I am called to live. His mind never wandered during lengthy synagogue prayers. He never pretended to be something he wasn't just to impress people. Instead, his heart was filled with perfect humility and submission to his Father's will, every second of every day of his life. That perfect, constant obedience is what is now credited to my account so that in the sight of God I am clothed with his perfect self-giving, not my own fake spirituality.

What is more, having died to pay the penalty that my sins deserved, Jesus was raised up for my justification. Just as the deaths of Ananias and Sapphira were the firstfruits of the judgment to come on the last day, so too the resurrection of Jesus from the dead is the firstfruits of the final resurrection (1 Cor. 15:20, 23). Jesus is the only one who has ever truly given his all to God. Even Barnabas, who sold his field and gave the proceeds to the apostles and later devoted his entire life to the ministry, was not completely sold out to God. Jesus is the only one who has completely humbled himself to the point of laying down his life utterly for his Father's glory and for our redemption. Just as the deaths of Ananias and Sapphira show that God takes sin seriously, so too the resurrection of Christ shows that God is satisfied with his payment in my place. His resurrection provides the proof that God has dealt with my sin once and for all at the cross, and now there is now no condemnation left for me. I am accepted by the Father because of the righteousness of the Son (Rom. 8:1). All I have to do is to trust my salvation to Christ.

That's why Scripture calls those who were being added to the church "those who believed in the Lord" (Acts 5:14). Believing in the Lord is not just believing in God's existence. Those who heard the apostles' message were mainly Jews who already believed in God's existence. There was more to it than that. What they believed was the message that Peter had preached in Acts 4: that this Jesus, who had been crucified in Jerusalem shortly before, had been raised from the dead and had thereby gained the power to heal our deepest disease of all, our sin sickness (Acts 4:10–12). They cast their hearts onto that hope as the only place under heaven in which to find salvation.

Has the Lord added you to his church? I'm not asking whether you are a regular attender at a place of worship. Going to church regularly is good, but it isn't what saves you. I'm asking whether you have believed in the Lord, resting your salvation entirely on his death in your place and placing your hope of heaven entirely on his resurrection for you. Is Christ's righteousness your only plea on the day when you will stand before God? Are you, in fact, a Christian? If not, then like Ananias and Sapphira, your death is certain. Whether you have sinned just as they did or in ways different from them, the poison of sin will have its ultimate effect in you. The only question is how long it will take to kill you. There is no way of escape other than Christ, whether you live to be nine or ninety.

Flee to Christ: Flee repeatedly to Christ and praise him for his love and grace that have the power to cure the deepest effects of the ancient serpent's bite. See the seriousness of your sin and praise him for his perfect righteousness that merits eternal life for you in heaven, instead of the death that you richly deserve. Ask God to show you your sin clearly so you can confess and repent of it moment by moment and day by day. Thank Jesus for paying the price for each and every one of your sins and wrapping you up irreversibly in his perfect goodness. Ask the Holy Spirit for growing strength and obedience to fight sin, and growing humility and dependence to be able to endure your weakness. How wonderful that people like you and me should now be invited in with those blessed words: "There is no condemnation for you, my son.

There is no condemnation for you, my daughter. All your sin has been paid for in Jesus's name! His righteousness has covered your nakedness. His death has purchased your life!" Praise God with a heart that is made whole in Christ, and sing with gratitude for the grace of God that grants life to us death-deserving sinners.

9

Suffering with Joy

Acts 5:17–42

NOBODY LIKES TRIALS. No one likes to suffer. Unless you are a masochist there is no pleasure in getting beaten up. Yet some people—both in the Bible and in church history—seem to have an ability to stand up to persecution. They seem able to handle whatever the world throws at them without backing down. They stand strong in the face of great pressure to conform. What makes someone able to persevere under pressure? How were the apostles able to stand firm in the face of such great persecution?

When we read Bible passages or stories from church history about persecution, there are two common mistakes that it's easy to make. On the one hand, we may trivialize the immense challenge of persecution and think to ourselves, "No problem! Bring it on! I could do that." On the other, we may be overwhelmed by fear and think to ourselves, "I could never sustain that kind of pressure. If persecution were to come, I would immediately fold." The problem with both perspectives is that we are looking at ourselves in isolation, without reference to God—and our lives are never actually lived that way. Whether we succeed or fail is ultimately governed by God's good purpose in our lives. Either he strengthens us to stand in order to demonstrate his power at work in us or he leaves us to ourselves to fail in order to show us our continuing weakness. Either way, he is always at work for his good purposes in us and through us. God is sovereign even over persecution and over our ability to stand or fall. With that thought firmly in mind, let's look at this passage in Acts 5 so that you and I can learn how we, too, may keep the faith in the face of trials and opposition.

Escalating Opposition

The first thing to notice from this passage is that the persecution of the early church is steadily escalating. This is not the first time that the apostles have been in trouble for the sake of the name of Jesus. In chapter 4 they were arrested and jailed briefly and then threatened and released (Acts 4:18–21). But the opposition to the gospel message among the Jewish authorities is hardening as the impact of the church is increasing. This is one of the basic truths of the spiritual conflict in which we find ourselves. Persecution often goes hand in hand with God's blessing. The person or the church that is ineffective in impacting a culture or community with the message of Jesus rarely receives much opposition. Nobody persecutes a fish that swims with the stream. But the more clearly you stand up for the truth of the gospel, the more you insist on proclaiming the life that is found in Christ alone, the more likely it is that you will face enmity.

Though the persecution of these early believers is increasing in strength, it is nonetheless still limited in its power. Most of the twelve apostles will end up being executed by the enemies of the church. That's a sobering thought. But they are not dead yet, even though their enemies would gladly see them so. Until God's work for each of them is complete, they are completely invulnerable. The enemies of God can arrest the apostles and put them in prison under lock and key in guarded cells, but they have no power to keep them there if God chooses to release them (Acts 5:19–21). No doors can stay locked when God determines to open them. Nor is this the only case in which God frees his people from prison by supernatural means. Later in the book of Acts he will send an angel to bring Peter out of prison (12:6–17) and an earthquake to release Paul and Silas (16:25–34). The persecutor's power always extends just as far as God allows it to go and no further. In this chapter, we see the rather humorous picture of the Sanhedrin sending to the prison to bring the captives to trial, only to discover that they are not there (5:21–22). What made it even worse for the enemies of the gospel was the fact that the apostles were already back in the temple doing precisely what they had been arrested for, preaching the name of Christ (5:25)!

If you want to see just how hard it is to shut these people up, all you have to do is look at what happens when their persecutors finally do bring them in front of the Sanhedrin. The chief priest reminds them that they had already been warned to stop preaching about Jesus, yet here they are still filling Jerusalem with this teaching and charging the Jewish leaders with being responsible for Jesus's death (Acts 5:28). Peter's response begins by denying that the Sanhedrin has the right to bind the apostles' consciences in that way: they have to obey God rather than men. This is a clear escalation of Peter's statement to the Jewish authorities back in 4:19, which he posed in the form of a rhetorical question: "Whether it is right in the sight of God to listen to you rather than to God, you must judge." Now his reply has become a simple statement of fact: "We must obey God rather than men" (5:29).

Holy Boldness

Most of us, even if we were not silenced by such opposition, would at least become more cautious in how and where we proclaimed the gospel. Not so the apostles! Peter proceeds to repeat the offense right in front of the eyes of his opponents. He declares once again before them precisely the same gospel message that he has been in trouble for proclaiming: "The God of our fathers raised Jesus, whom you killed by hanging him on a tree. God exalted him at his right hand as Leader and Savior, to give repentance to Israel and forgiveness of sins" (Acts 5:30–31). Peter does not back down at all from delivering God's message, even in such a hostile environment. No wonder the Sanhedrin wants to put him to death immediately!

Assistance comes for the apostles from a strange quarter—Gamaliel the Pharisee. Gamaliel argues against executing them (Acts 5:35–39). Instead he tells the Sanhedrin members to leave the apostles alone and see what happens. If these men are simply proclaiming a human idea, Gamaliel argues, they will not succeed. But if they are truly from God, and you oppose them, he says, you will be found to be opposing God.

This argument from Gamaliel may sound very reasonable to our modern pluralistic society, but it is a very unusual position for a religious leader to take in the ancient world, particularly a Pharisee. It certainly isn't the majority view among the Pharisees, as can be seen by the fact that Gamaliel's own student, Saul of Tarsus, is leading the drive to execute Christians as soon as Acts 8:1.

The reality that not everybody on the Sanhedrin is entirely convinced by Gamaliel's argument can be seen by the fact that they don't simply let the apostles go to see what will happen; they first beat them and further charge them not to speak in the name of Jesus (Acts 5:40). Yet Gamaliel's speech is enough to preserve the lives of the apostles for now. Once again we see God's ability to use unexpected means to accomplish his own purposes.

The apostles' response to this heightened persecution is to rejoice (Acts 5:41)! That is truly bizarre. They leave the council rejoicing that they have been counted worthy to suffer dishonor for the name of Christ. Not only do they rejoice, but they continue undaunted, day by day, publicly and privately, in the temple and from house to house, teaching and preaching Jesus as the Christ (5:42). Neither threats of violence nor actual violence can deter them from telling everyone they meet about Jesus.

The Inevitability of Persecution

From the experience of the apostles we may learn that persecution is inevitable if we are really living the Christian life. We talked in the last chapter about Satan's three strategies: persecution, seduction, and deception. We may anticipate assaults from all three of these directions, but perhaps Satan's favorite strategy is persecution. It is not necessarily his most effective strategy since, as the church father Tertullian put it, "the blood of the martyrs is the seed of the church,"[1] but I think it is the one he enjoys most. As a result, we may each expect to face persecution in some form or other. In the American context, we may rarely be called on to put our lives on the line for the Lord, as the apostles were; we are perhaps unlikely to be beaten up for our faith, although Christians around the world continue to face that reality daily. But we will certainly face mockery, insults, and sneers from the world. The more open we are about our faith, the more we exist outside the cozy confines of the church, the more such treatment will become a reality for us. As Paul tells Timothy in 2 Timothy 3:12, "All who desire to live a godly life in Christ Jesus will be persecuted."

The easiest way to avoid persecution is to conform to and fit in with the world, at least outwardly. You can avoid or minimize persecution by privatizing your faith, keeping your religion to yourself, and acting as if matters of faith aren't that important in the real world. It would have been easy for the apostles to have stayed within the safe confines of the group of those who were already Christians, having their Bible studies secretly in a safe house somewhere. The authorities might then have looked in the other direction. That wasn't the apostles' way. They took their message out into the temple, into the marketplace of ideas. They would not be safely shut away.

How often do you or I run the risk of persecution by saying something or by being willing to go out in public with our faith? For most of us, the answer is "Not very often." We need to hear the challenge of Acts 5:17–42 and be willing to take the gospel to the streets and into our relationships, seeking regularly to share it "in season and out of season," as Paul tells Timothy (2 Tim. 4:2). I find that admonition personally challenging because I always seem to be waiting for the gospel to be "in season"; that is, I want to wait until people broach the topic, ask a question, or in some other way signal an openness to

1 Tertullian, *Apology*, in Tertullian, Minucius Felix, *Apology. De Spectaculis. Minucius Felix: Octavius*, trans. T. R. Glover and Gerald H. Rendall, Loeb Classical Library 250 (Harvard University Press, 1931), 226–27.

hear the good news. But the apostles were very bold with their "out of season" declaration of the gospel as well—even in the hostile setting of the Sanhedrin.

Now it is true that some people are vocal about their faith in an entirely obnoxious way. They are sure to be persecuted, not because they are being faithful so much as because they are being unnecessarily offensive. This passage is not a call to be obnoxious, but it is a call to be public, faithful, and direct about our testimony. The apostles don't regard bearing witness to the gospel as a matter of personal choice or temperament. They tell the Sanhedrin that they must obey God rather than men, that God has made them witnesses of the death and resurrection of Christ and the life that comes to us through these things (Acts 5:32).

If you are a Christian, God has made you, too, a witness to his power, grace, and love. Can we remain silent about these things? Can we fail to bring before people the need for repentance and the forgiveness of sins that comes only through faith in Christ? God's command rings in our ears: "Go therefore and make disciples of all nations . . . , teaching them to observe all that I have commanded you" (Matt. 28:18–20). That's not just a message for the apostles; it has implications for all of us in our own contexts and situations. Being a witness to Christ is not an optional extra in the Christian life, an elective module for those entrusted with a special gift of evangelism. It is a calling, a command to every man and woman, boy and girl. If you have experienced the grace of God that comes through the power of the Spirit, you are a witness.

The Essence of Our Message

To what events, though, are we witnesses? What is the essence of our message? It's important that we know the answer to that question; otherwise our words will be wasted. If you have ever engaged people in conversation about Christ, you know how easy it is to be distracted and get off topic. Is the Bible true? What about creation and evolution? What about the place of men and women in the church? What about homosexuality? There are a thousand and one things that we can discuss with people, many of them profitable and good topics in themselves, some of them perhaps necessary to prepare the way for the gospel—but nonetheless not themselves reaching to the heart of the matter. We need to learn from Peter how to cut to the heart in our conversations.

Peter had a central message about Christ that he wanted to deliver at every possible opportunity that presented itself (Acts 5:30–31). It is this: Jesus Christ is the one whom God has chosen and sent. He died on the cross, but God raised him from the dead, exalting him as Lord and Savior. He has come to give repentance and forgiveness of sins.

Peter's message is the gospel in a nutshell. Jesus Christ, God's Messiah, came to earth, lived a perfect life, and died on the cross as a substitute for his people. He didn't stay dead, for God raised him up. You, too, can have the new life he came to bring if you come to him and repent; that is, if you ask God to forgive you your sins and grant you a new and different life. All his people will ultimately be with Jesus where he is in heaven now, for by faith they are united to him in an unbreakable way. There is no other way to enjoy God's favor forever. This is what we are witnesses of as his people—in company with the Holy Spirit, the witness who has the power to change the hardest heart (5:32). This message is the one we need to get out to a lost and dying world.

Not everyone will thank you for sharing the gospel message. The members of the Sanhedrin wanted to kill Peter when he told them the gospel (Acts 5:33). So also some of your friends and neighbors may not be thrilled to hear your testimony. But those whom God is drawing to himself, those whom God is adding to his church, will sooner or later respond to that message and come to faith in Christ. Our job is simply to sow the seeds wherever we can, not agonize endlessly about whether those seeds are individually bearing fruit.

God's Plan for Persecution

Persecution is not part of our existence here as Christians just because Satan delights to torment us. As I said earlier, Satan has no power to touch you beyond what God gives. Those who insult you and assault you would have no power to do so unless God allowed them, just as the ravenous lions were totally unable to touch Daniel in the lion's den (Dan. 6). So why don't we all receive the Daniel treatment and get delivered from our enemies? Why does Peter get released here, courtesy of Gamaliel's speech, while Stephen gets stoned to death a couple of chapters later, as witnessed approvingly by Gamaliel's student (Acts 8:1; cf. 22:3)? Did Stephen somehow blow his gospel presentation and not get the words right? Was it because Stephen had missed his quiet time that morning?

Not at all. Persecution is part of God's will for the church. There's a fascinating passage in Revelation 6 in which John sees those who have been martyred for the faith crying out to God, "O Sovereign Lord, holy and true, how long before you will judge and avenge our blood on those who dwell on the earth?" (Rev. 6:10). You might think the answer would be that the martyrs need to wait a little longer because there are still more people to be saved. You might think that is why God continues to exercise patience with the wicked. This is true enough; Peter says so in 2 Peter 3:9. But it is not the answer given to the martyrs in the book of Revelation. Rather, they are told to be patient, to wait a little longer until the full number of their fellow servants has been martyred (Rev. 6:11). God's purpose in this world is fulfilled not simply in spite of persecution and martyrdom but through persecution and martyrdom.

Once again the gospel turns our natural logic on its head. We think instinctively that if God loves us and has a wonderful plan for our lives, it can't possibly be his will for something bad like persecution to happen to us. In that case, however, we have a hard time explaining the history of the church around the world, which is in large measure a history of persecution. I once visited a Shinto shrine in Nagoya, Japan, which had been erected on the spot where a group of Christians were massacred in the seventeenth century. As part of the shrine, which was built as an act of atonement by the persecutors, there is a little museum with artifacts from the period, including the edicts outlawing Christianity and a "fumier," a brass plate with a picture of Christ that Christians were forced to step on as an act of renouncing their faith, on pain of death. It was a moving experience to go through this museum. Why didn't God step in and rescue those believers from their painful fate? His refusal to do so doesn't make sense if God's plan for our lives is for us always to be comfortable and happy.

In reality, the Bible and church history show us that God loves us and has a wonderful plan for the glory of his own name, which is far and away the best purpose for our lives. God wants people's eyes to be opened to his glory, and that happens when people see men and women who count obedience to God as more valuable than their personal comfort, reputation, and even life itself. How can you be lashed with whips to within an inch of your life, as the apostles were, and still go away rejoicing that you are counted worthy to suffer for the name of Jesus? You can't if your own interests are at the center of your universe. If you view religion as a means to get what you want, whether what you want is a comfortable life now or a safe ticket to a pleasant eternity in the good place, you will never understand the apostles' rejoicing while they are being persecuted. If you are serving God for what he can do for you, then you will be disappointed and downcast, perhaps even destroyed, by the experience of persecution.

But if you understand the depths of your own sin and depravity, if you understand the amazing depth of God's love in reaching down to you, then you are on the right track. If you understand that Jesus Christ, in order to save you, was not only willing to be beaten within an inch of his life and to be crowned with thorns, he was willing to be crucified and cut off from the life-giving presence of the Father because of your sins, then the mystery of joy in the midst of persecution starts to become clearer. If you start to understand the depths of God's love for you in the gospel, then the glory of the God who has loved you this much will take on a kind of radioactive glow that will suffuse your whole life. His glory will become the only thing that matters: not your comfort, success, riches, or even your life. Now your trials and persecutions are no longer necessary evils; they instead become opportunities to shout aloud your love for him. If the gospel is really true, and if its truth has really grasped you, then you will see suffering for the sake of the name of Christ as truly glorious.

Moreover, the beautiful grace of the gospel is at its most glorious in the fact that it is sufficient not merely for bold apostles who stand firm in their faith in the midst of persecution, but also for weak believers who often fudge and fail. Even Peter, who was so bold in this moment, did not always stand up strongly for the truth of the gospel. This is the same Peter who earlier denied that he even knew Jesus (Luke 22:54–62), the same Peter who would back away from the Gentile believers in Antioch when he came under pressure from the Judaizers (Gal. 2:11–14). That is the most astounding thing about the Christian message. We are not saved by our ability to rejoice in the face of persecution. The gospel does not rest on our personal faithfulness under fire: it is rooted and grounded in Christ's perfect faithfulness under fire in our place. On the last day, when we stand before the ultimate Judge, whose decisions transcend any and every human tribunal, the question will not be, "How faithful were you when persecution came along in your life?" It will be, "What is your relationship to Christ, who suffered perfectly under persecution in your place?" He never backed down under fire. He pressed ahead even to the point of death on the cross and the hellish darkness of separation from his Father so that we might be justified in him on that day. In this perfect righteousness of Christ is all our hope, as very weak and often cowardly believers.

God's Glory in Our Weakness

Finally, remember that it is in our weakness and sufferings that God's glory and strength is made most clearly manifest. What is the most compelling evidence that the apostolic movement was from God and not from man? Was it the thousands who flocked to join the early church on the day of Pentecost? That was impressive, but great speakers have often drawn large crowds. Was it that the apostles were willing to die for the cause? That was impressive too, but many have mistakenly died for what they believed in. Theudas and Judas the Galilean, the two revolutionaries whom Gamaliel mentions, died for their cause, but no one remembers them now (Acts 5:36–37). What made the Christians most powerful was that as often as their enemies killed them, more and more of them kept springing up. In the midst of their manifold weakness—their lack of political influence and educational pedigree and money and resources, even the sin that dogged all the early churches—they continued to grow and grow. Gamaliel was certainly right: the only explanation for that movement was that God was with them and his purposes were being accomplished by his strength.

Our churches should be similarly inexplicable—not in terms of our overwhelming size, wealth, and strength but in our rejoicing in persecution and suffering for the sake of Jesus. We should be inexplicable in our commitment to God even when things do not go well for us in life and in the church, and in constantly repenting and looking to Jesus as our only hope when we fail and let him down yet again. We should be so much in love with the Lord Jesus, because of the love he has shown us in the gospel, that nothing he could ask of us would ever be too much. We, too, are called to have an undeniable, unmistakable passion about everything that we do that flows out of an overwhelming and overwhelmed love for God. To the extent that we begin to radiate that witness—in the midst of all our weakness and messiness—the world will begin to see the glory of God made manifest in our midst also.

10

The Gospel and the Poor

Acts 4:32–35; 6:1–7

WHEN OUR CHILDREN were growing up, they had a couple of books based on the characters from a TV show called *Fraggle Rock*. For those of you too young to have watched this cinematic masterpiece, there were essentially two distinct species living in a symbiotic harmony in this mythical place: the Doozers and the Fraggles. The Doozers were little creatures who wore hard hats and were constantly active, working on tiny building projects made entirely out of radish sticks, with no visible purpose except the joy of accomplishing a task. Little Doozers worked very conscientiously at school and looked forward to the day when they could finally get their hard hats and join a construction team. Meanwhile, Fraggles liked to dance, sing, and yell, "Whoopee!" very loud. They brought the important element of fun and laughter to the Doozers' otherwise rather gray, serious, even joyless existence. In addition, they contributed an essential element to the ecology of Fraggle Rock by consuming the Doozers' constructions so that there would constantly be room for them to build new things.

One purpose of this "interspecies" interaction on the television series was to teach children the most fundamental kindergarten lesson of all: that even though we are very different from one another, we need each another and contribute our different gifts to society. The temptation for each of us is to assume that our particular gift mix is of primary value. Speaking personally as a Class A Doozer, it is easy for people like me to assume that we are the ones who really make the world go round. Fraggles may be useful for entertainment purposes when you need a little fun, but when there is work to be done the world really needs Doozers. That was precisely the outlook of the family I grew up in, which was deeply judgmental of Fraggles. As a result I all too often still share that sinful outlook: I tend to treat celebrating the good things in life as an optional extra and Fraggles as unnecessary impediments to getting the job done.

Meanwhile, Fraggles (you know who you are) tend to regard Doozers as altogether too serious and somber. "You need to lighten up," they say. "There's more to life than studying, building, and organizing schedules and rosters. You need to have a party once in a while. Be thankful and celebrate God's good gifts for once—instead of always seeing the glass as not only half empty but in dire need of being filled up." Perhaps we should all read those *Fraggle Rock* books again.

Diversity is present in the church as well as in individuals. Presbyterians like me are often found among the Doozers of the ecclesiastical world. We are the Christians who like everything done decently and in order, according to a Confession of Faith thirty chapters long and a Book of Church Order twice that size. Meanwhile, our charismatic brothers and sisters are perhaps at the Fraggle end of the spectrum, with their emphasis on the immediate work of the Holy Spirit, an emphasis that leads to celebrative worship and spontaneity. On both sides we search for proof texts in the Bible that seem to justify our characteristic tendencies: we seek to show that real Christians should be organized Doozers or spontaneous Fraggles. But the amazing thing about the Scriptures in general, and the book of Acts in particular, is that God is not easily put in a box that matches our individual or group temperaments. As we will see in this passage in Acts 6, the early church was constantly remarkable for its ability to bring and hold together things that we tend to see as warring opposites.

The Work of the Spirit and Planning

The first of these opposing pairs is the work of the Holy Spirit on the one hand and careful organization and planning on the other. In the church these are often seen as opposites, but in the book of Acts they appear side by side. The Spirit is the one who builds the church in the book of Acts, often by means of dramatic signs and wonders; yet at the same time the apostles apply intensely practical wisdom to the problems of ministry to the poor (Acts 6:1–4). They observe the need to ensure fairness in dividing out the food that is being given to the widows and the poor of different ethnic groups in the community, and they solve this problem by appointing a committee—or, better, a ministry team—to organize the work. These leaders are to be men of character and wisdom, men who have skills that commend them for that task, but they are also to be men who are filled with the Spirit (6:4). Human skill together with the divine Spirit, practical wisdom combined with divine anointing: these are the qualifications they need for their task.

You see the same combination of the regular and the remarkable in God's deliverance of the apostles in the previous chapter. The first time the apostles are arrested and put into prison, God uses a remarkable deliverance to set them free: the angel of the Lord opens the doors of the jail and brings them out (5:19). Yet when they are immediately hauled back in before the Sanhedrin, which is ready to kill them—instead of sending another angel from heaven to deliver them, this time the Lord sends a Pharisee, Gamaliel, whose reasoned argument saves their lives (5:34–39). Remarkable and ordinary providence work together, hand in hand, side by side.

How is God at work in your life and mine? We tend to be preprogrammed to expect God to work in certain ways and not in others.

Fraggles

Some of us are always looking for God to work in spectacular ways. We want God to heal us dramatically; we find it hard to believe it is really God at work if our healing involves regular medicine and doctors. We want God to show us our future spouse through some crazy providential encounter; we can't believe that it could happen simply through the mundane application of human wisdom—getting to know members of the opposite sex who exude godly character and wisdom and figuring out which of them is a good fit. We want God to convert our friends and family through some dramatic sign; we are impatient with the slow work of living the Christian life in front of them. We want to know the time and date for our own conversions; we resist simply acknowledging that "once I was blind but now I see." The reality is that God often works in our lives and in the lives of others through ordinary means, and we should be as ready to recognize these displays of his power as the more dramatic interventions.

Doozers

Others of us, though, are so programmed to expect God only to work through normal, humanly explicable circumstances that we have a hard time believing that he will ever do anything outside the box. This is where I often find myself. We may not actually deny that there is such a person as the Holy Spirit, but we don't expect him ever to surprise us. We may spend hours on evangelistic training programs and sermon preparation, trusting in these means instead of in the Lord. When problems arise, our instinctive approach is to organize our way out of them rather than to pray our way through them. We plan our whole lives out to the nth degree, leaving little room for the unscheduled activities that God has in mind for us. We need to recognize that God is still living and active today, and he delights to surprise us and to do far more abundantly than all we can ask or imagine (Eph. 3:20).

Now to be sure, we should not expect our experience in the church today to match that of the book of Acts. As we said earlier, the signs of the book of Acts are just that: signs that in Jesus Christ the kingdom of God has indeed arrived. They are firstfruits of the final consummation, that day when every knee will bow before the Lord and every tear will be wiped away from our eyes. Just as the Lord did not miraculously heal most of the lame men in Jerusalem in his own day, so too his normal pattern of interaction with his people today does not involve dramatic healing miracles. Yet I think that we Presbyterians sometimes too quickly assume that our prayers are merely an optional extra to the medicine that really heals people, instead of bringing our needs before God with real boldness of faith. What is more, the things that we consider ordinary—repentance, conversion, baby steps of change—are actually great works of God's power. Our gifts of administration, order, and planning are good, but they are no substitute for the work of God. The church needs both—and it especially needs leaders who combine the filling of the Holy Spirit with the skills of wisdom and competent organization so that the needs of God's people may be met. We should be praying for our elders and deacons to have both giftings.

Ministry to the Poor and Faithfulness to the Gospel

The second set of apparent opposites that the book of Acts holds together is the combination of an amazing ministry to the poor on the one hand and faithfulness to the gospel on the other. This hasn't always been problematic for the church. The Roman emperor Julian the Apostate (AD 331–363) wrote, "It is disgraceful that when . . . the impious Galileans [that is, the Christians] support not only their poor, but ours as well, everyone can see that our people lack aid from us."[1] Yet in the twentieth century these two priorities diverged, as liberals embraced the social gospel and focused on the needs of the poor to the exclusion of the gospel, while evangelicals often focused on the gospel to the exclusion of ministry to the poor. There are moves today to bridge the divide and to bring the gospel back together with a concern for the poor, but some Christian people are deeply suspicious of the dangers of this kind of ministry. They are concerned that any church that ministers to the poor is necessarily going to lose its focus on the gospel and become simply a social-work agency.

1 Julian, "Letter 22: To Arsacius, High-Priest of Galatia," in *Letters. Epigrams. Against the Galilaeans. Fragments*, trans. Wilmer C. Wright, Loeb Classical Library 157 (Harvard University Press, 1923), 67.

This passage in the book of Acts, along with the lessons of church history, make it clear that the existence of a merely social gospel is indeed a valid and serious concern. It is possible for churches—and especially for pastors—to lose focus on what is of first priority: the proclamation of the gospel. The apostles see that danger and guard themselves carefully against it, insisting that they have to devote their time to pursuing their primary calling, which is the ministry of the word and of prayer (6:4). Yet at the same time, they don't ignore the needs of the community in which they find themselves. There were poor people all around them who desperately needed financial and other assistance. In particular, those widows who had become Christians were cut off from the financial support that they had formerly received from the synagogue. These were real needs, and the apostles recognized them by delegating those tasks to people who were well-qualified to meet them, men who were filled with the Holy Spirit and wisdom. In that way, ministry to the poor and the clear preaching of the gospel didn't have to be polar opposites. By having different groups of people overseeing different aspects of ministry, they were able to maintain focus on the gospel and still meet the needs of the people.

The same should be true in the contemporary church: We need to have leaders who are devoted to the ministry of the word and prayer, and we need others who give themselves to practical matters and the needs of the poor. Indeed, the structure of the Presbyterian church is designed on precisely this model, especially as it is laid out in Paul's letters to Timothy. The pastor and other elders are entrusted with the oversight of the church and the ministry of the word and prayer (1 Tim. 2:1; 2 Tim. 4:2). Preaching is hard work; it takes education, preparation, thought, and prayer if it is to be done well—for the glory of God, for the edification of believers, and in order to bring the gospel to those who have not yet heard it. Elders share actively in overseeing the congregation pastorally, encouraging those who need to be encouraged and challenging those who need to be challenged. The session of the church, which is made up of the pastor and elders, is not merely a management committee for the church. It is a spiritual leadership team, made up of the men whom God has gifted and called to that task. Alongside the session, Presbyterian churches also have a board of deacons whose function is to oversee many of the practical needs of the church, especially ministry to the poor and needy (see 1 Tim. 3). As they devote themselves to these functions, the elders are freed up to do what they are called to do, and the body operates effectively.

Concern for the Poor

The result of the church leadership structure described in the New Testament ought to be that we have an effective ministry to the poor and needy in our community, beginning with those who are inside the church (Gal. 6:10). Why should we be so concerned for the poor? The answer is that God is concerned for the poor, and he invites us to share his concern. The gospel is all about God's love that provides for the needs of those who have nothing: our most profound poverty is spiritual, which God answers by sending his own Son. But Jesus didn't merely come to meet our spiritual needs; he also fed the hungry, cured the blind, and healed the sick.

So too we are called to love our neighbor (Lev. 19:18), which surely involves being concerned for their physical needs. This care may be as simple as cooking meals for someone who is sick or helping people move. Sometimes this care may involve financial help—but it will always be more than merely a financial handout. God didn't merely rescue us from a safe distance, writing a check to cover our spiritual debt; he got personally involved in our lives. His love for us centers on his desire for relationship with us: he wants to be our God and have us as his people. Jesus didn't just feed people; he always preached the good news of a Father in heaven who was concerned about them and wanted to watch over them as his sheep. Our concern for others, too, should center in a desire for relationship: we don't just want to help people with their immediate needs; we want to come to know people and especially for them to know our God. As a result, the gospel always goes hand in hand with our help. We are called not merely to fix our neighbor's problems but to love our neighbor, which always involves the goal of relationship, both with us and with God. The goal is always real relationship, not simply befriending the other person as an evangelism project, hoping to score another notch in our Bible.

My first pastoral call was a church plant in a very poor area of Oxford, England. There we tended people's yards, ministered to street children, fed the whole church each week, and regularly visited the local school. Because the needs were many, the opportunities for the gospel were many. We had relationships with kids, families, social workers, and teachers. We lived among the people and sought to befriend them where they were, earning the right to share the good news of Jesus with them. Our greatest joy was to see men and women, boys and girls, come to faith in Christ.

This is where the help that the church can give people is so much more powerful than the help that the state can give. People have needs for many different reasons: Some are poor because of age or disability, while others are poor because of youth or irresponsibility. Some have a temporary, short-term need; others will be in need until they die. Love enables us to minister to people in a way that fits their particular needs. For example, an older lady may need someone to help with her utility costs. But love recognizes that perhaps she also needs someone to sit with her and keep her company. An alcoholic may have a hard time finding a job. But love also recognizes that there is a deeper problem that needs to be addressed and that a simple handout cannot fix, a problem that needs ongoing counseling and support. Love can speak the truth boldly and gently. Sometimes really helping someone means saying no to their request, for to give them what they want would simply be to feed their brokenness, not to help them to face up to it.

What is more, love cares enough to see that all people have the same fundamental problem, however rich or poor they may be in the things of this world. That problem is our spiritual poverty. By nature we are all destitute before God. If we are genuinely going to help anyone we will need to point them toward the hope that can be found only in Christ and to the spiritual community that can be found only in the church. Peoples' needs are not simply problems to be solved but opportunities to communicate the gospel to people who are profoundly broken, spiritually as well as materially. Yet it is difficult to communicate God's eternal care to someone if we don't also care about their immediate need for food, for shelter, or for a friend to talk to. Practical diaconal ministry and the gospel belong together.

Jews and Gentiles

The third odd couple that we find united in the portion of Acts that we are examining are the Jews and Gentiles who are brought together in one church. The widows who are being overlooked in the food distribution are specifically Hellenistic Jews, from the Greek-speaking community in Jerusalem, while the Aramaic-speaking widows are being taken care of (Acts 6:1). It is interesting to see how the church resolves the issue. They don't require all the widows to learn Hebrew. Nor do they broker a compromise in which the smaller, Greek-speaking community is given an appropriate proportional representation on the new deacon board to ensure equal rights for all. Two or three Greek-speaking deacons would be fair, you might think. I don't think that solution would necessarily be wrong, but in this case they adopt a radically countercultural solution. All seven of the protodeacons have Greek names, including one, Nicolaus, who is a convert to Judaism from Gentile Antioch (6:5–6). What is more, these men are chosen by the community, not by the apostles. All seven are united in being filled with the Spirit and wisdom, so the community trusts them to act fairly, even though all of them are Gentiles.

This is a mark of the impact that the gospel already has on the whole community of believers. As well as bringing their possessions and sharing them to meet the needs of others (4:32–35), the early Christians are also willing to put their personal rights on hold to make sure that the needs of their brothers and sisters in the minority community are being met. No wonder the preaching of the gospel flourishes in Jerusalem when it is backed up by a community that lives it out in such a powerful way! It is striking that Luke here mentions specifically that "many priests" become believers (6:7). Perhaps this large number is due to the fact that the priests are in charge of the temple's ministry to the poor and so are the ones most in a position to see just how radically different the early church community is in their approach to the destitute.

Implications for Today

What would it look like for us to be this kind of caring, inclusive, self-sacrificing community in our context, first for the sake of the family of believers and then for the wider population? To begin with we should be praying specifically for the Lord to open up doors that will show us the good works that he has prepared for us (Eph. 2:10). This begins with keeping our eyes open for needs among ourselves that we can meet, and then it broadens out to the needs of our neighbors and those around us whom the Lord brings across our path. Sometimes people will tell us what their needs are, but often we will have to ask them. If, like me, you find yourself naturally blind toward people in need, then you will need to ask God for a heart of compassion that cares deeply for people—and for eyes that see their needs. If, on the other hand, you are inclined toward a "savior complex" and are tempted to jump in and be a rescuer of everyone around you, you may need to ask the Lord for more discernment about who he is bringing to you for help, along with what real help would look like in a given situation. If we have eyes to see, we will often recognize needs that we cannot possibly meet ourselves. Yet we can still pray for those needy people and ask that the God who is able to do far more abundantly than all we can organize and plan would meet their needs through the power of his Holy Spirit.

Second, we should be praying that God would add to our number those who have specific giftedness in the area of ministry to the poor who might become deacons. These are not simply the people who do the work of diaconal ministry but rather those who encourage and organize the gifts of the body in this area. Since it is a service function rather than a leadership role (in fact, the Greek word for "deacon" simply means "servant"), diaconal ministry in this broader sense appropriately—even necessarily—involves the gifts of women as well as men, whether or not we choose to use the title "deaconess" to describe them. Certainly in 1 Timothy 3:11 Paul recognizes the importance of a group of women who ministered alongside the deacons. We should pray that the Lord would give us godly men and women with a heart for this service and with the gifts to help us all become involved in a deeper way with the needs of our community.

Third, we need to share the early church's passion for placing the needs and concerns of others ahead of our own, especially across racial and cultural divides. The Jewish believers didn't campaign for their fair share of places on the deacon board; they were happy to see it entirely made up of Hellenistic believers because they put the needs of the community ahead of their own needs. Yet we sometimes evaluate churches by how well they meet our personal needs or how they cater to our interests. Do they play our kind of music? Do they attract the kind of people we want to spend time with? Do we feel comfortable with the style of service? Are there people like us who go there? These things matter, to be sure, but the deeper questions of substance often go unasked because we are approaching the church as consumers looking for the church that will give us the greatest reward for our donations. In contrast, the early church put the needs of others first, in order that the new community might be a place of genuine diversity and so that others from very different backgrounds might be won for Christ. This can be challenging to work out in practice, of course, but we have to start with a genuine desire to reach across racial, political, and social divides to make those who are different from us feel especially welcome.

Finally, we should see how this passage challenges each of our hearts. I know that by nature I don't think enough of the practical needs of others or how to put the preferences of others ahead of my own. I don't love people as I should, and so in consequence I don't go through life weighed down with their burdens. It is very easy for me to blow people off and find excuses as to why I don't have to help them or care about them. I'm too busy; it's not my gifting; like the Doozers, I have endless towers of radish sticks to construct. I want to have things my way all the time; I don't want to have to put up with those who have different perspectives, outlooks, or cultural backgrounds. Perhaps you are like me. You are afraid that getting involved in ministry to needy people will consume you. Yet this passage in the book of Acts shows us that our lack of concern for others puts us out of step with God and out of step with the gospel. The apostles understood that God is concerned about people, even poverty-stricken foreign widows who had no lands or possessions to contribute to the church. God is concerned about people whom the world around us would judge to be takers and not givers, a worthless irrelevance that would get in the way of building a successful church. We too need to learn to love those who are outcasts and aliens, those who are considered the last, the least, and the lost in our society. We desperately need God's help to confront our apathy and to try to love others with wisdom.

Many years ago, in our ministry in a needy part of Oxford, England, we saw God answer those prayers for compassion as people reached outside their comfort zone. Each Sunday, our small church community all ate together, and I vividly remember a vegetarian browning ground beef for the lunch. I saw people choose to sit next to and embrace people with lice visible in their hair. I saw a former alcoholic, a group of street kids, an illiterate single mother, and an elderly lady who grew up living on a canal boat, alongside postgraduate students at the university and our young family, forming a community of love for one another and for the gospel. The gospel really is good news for the poor—which in spiritual terms is every single one of us!

Yet the challenge posed by ministry to the poor is real. Ministry always exposes our idolatries. Whether we naturally avoid helping because we want to preserve our own comfort or whether we dive right in over our heads because we love to feel significant and we get a self-righteous kick out of our sacrifice—either way our actions may be more about fulfilling our own needs than truly loving others.

The Gospel and the Poor

So how do you grow in genuine love for people who may be unattractive, undeserving, and needy, whom the world judges to be worthless? How do you care for people who may be ungrateful and entitled in response to your kindness? It all comes back to the gospel. Jesus could so easily have gone through all eternity without troubling himself about my needs. He could have sentenced me to a well-deserved doom in hell without ever getting up from his heavenly armchair. But he didn't do that. Instead, he left his heavenly home and entered our world, choosing to be born as an ordinary member of a very impoverished community. He was homeless as a baby, and then became a refugee far from his home as a young child (Matt. 2:13–14). Since Joseph disappears early from the Gospel accounts, Jesus may possibly have grown up fatherless, faced with supporting his mother as a widow. Perhaps that is why Jesus understood the world of the poor and the outcast so well.

In his adult life Jesus faced a world of overwhelming physical needs and addressed many of them. He fed the hungry, healed the sick, and raised the dead. But more profoundly still he faced a world with an overwhelming spiritual need—namely, redemption from sin—and he addressed that need comprehensively. Through his death on the cross, Jesus paid the debt for our cold and uncaring hearts. He did so not merely to set an example that I should (but cannot) follow. Through his life of unequaled compassion Jesus accomplished a perfect record of love and care for the poor and the other that now covers you and me and enables us to stand uncondemned in the Father's presence in spite of our many failures in this area. His love for us is the perfect expression of love for someone who was utterly lost. His love challenges our desire for comfort, control, and significance. But it does so in a way that assures us of our safety and security in him, without leaving us crushed by guilt, failure, and shame. Only the gospel and the righteousness of Christ give us the gritty courage to face our own ugly sinfulness and joyfully turn to God for the help we need to grow and change. God has prepared for us times when we fail and see our weaknesses, and other times when we surprise ourselves, and we have loving thoughts and actions that are not characteristic to our own sinful flesh. The gospel is our only hope to grow in loving others with a spirit of honesty and humility.

As you and I behold the gospel and ponder God's love for the needy in Christ—his love for us—then our hearts will begin to be warmed toward one another and toward the world around us in a way that will compel us to love and care for our neighbors. The gospel doesn't normally call you to die for your neighbor; rather it calls you to the much harder task of living for him or her day after day. It calls you to build a relationship with your neighbors out of which you can know them and their needs and seek to serve them in whatever ways God has gifted and blessed you, while always pointing them to Christ. This is hard and sometimes frustrating work, and we will often fail to love people as we ought. Yet as we slowly grow in our love for the gospel and for our neighbors, the gospel will be more effectively preached in our community—both from the pulpit and in our day-to-day lives. People will be added to God's church from all different backgrounds, united as one in the love of Jesus Christ.

11

Preaching to the Deaf

Acts 6:8–7:60

HAVE YOU EVER HAD the experience of trying to share your faith with someone and not getting your words quite right? Perhaps you got sidetracked into a discussion of evolution or politics, or you just got tangled up in your own thoughts. You mangled your presentation, and the person went away totally unconvinced. That night you lay awake and rehearsed the whole argument, putting together just the right words, convinced that if you'd only said it better, then that person's mind would have been changed.

This passage in the book of Acts should forever cure you of that anxiety. To be sure, we should strive to be clear and faithful in our presentation of the gospel, but it is not a lack of clarity that is the main problem.

The Stephen we meet in Acts 6–7 is a profoundly effective witness for Jesus, one of the best evangelists in the history of the church. Luke describes him as a man full of grace and power, one who is "doing great wonders and signs among the people" (6:8). When Stephen enters into debates with opponents of the gospel, he shuts their mouths with the force of his arguments. No one can withstand the wisdom and the Spirit (that is, the Holy Spirit) with which he is speaking (6:10). Stephen gets his message right, and he gets it out, presenting the truth of the gospel with great clarity to many people in Jerusalem. You might think that everyone would have to be convinced by such a phenomenal presentation of the gospel, that thousands more would be added to the church.

If only we, too, could speak with such eloquence and power—surely our unsaved friends and family members would be transformed.

Think again. Clever words are not enough. Even wise words presented with the insight of the Holy Spirit are not enough. It is possible for hearts to be so closed to the gospel that even the truth presented as plainly, clearly, and winsomely as it could possibly be is not enough to open them. This is what it means for people to be "dead in . . . trespasses and sins," as Paul puts it (Eph. 2:1). When you're giving a message to a group that is eager to hear what you say, we call it "preaching to the choir." This passage shows us the opposite: Stephen was preaching to the obstinately deaf—or, perhaps more accurately, preaching to the spiritually dead.

Not only are Stephen's hearers not convinced by his proclamation of the gospel, but they are so enraged by it that they bring charges against him and drag him in front of the Sanhedrin, the Jewish council. They find people to claim falsely that Stephen has been speaking blasphemous words against Moses and against God (6:11), declaring that Jesus of Nazareth would destroy the temple and change the laws of Moses (6:14). The gospel of Christ is, in their minds, an assault on the central pillars of their religious faith: the temple and the law. The temple in Jerusalem is the place where God dwells in their midst, and the law of Moses is God's revelation of his character and purpose; thus far they are correct enough. But they miss the whole point of the law and the temple, both of which were designed by God to point forward to Jesus. Certainly those who accuse Stephen are under no illusion that Christianity is merely presenting an alternative way for everyone to come to the same God. They understand that you have to choose one way or the other: either Christianity or Judaism. That is why they drag Stephen off to face the religious authorities on the charge of disrespecting the temple and the law of Moses.

Defending the Faith

It would be a bit misleading to call Stephen's speech in front of the Sanhedrin a "defense." There is nothing apologetic about Stephen's apologetics. As Charles Spurgeon once said, "The gospel is like a lion. Who ever heard of defending a lion? Just turn it loose; it will defend itself."[1] That is what Stephen does in the passage we are examining. Instead of defending himself, Stephen takes the offensive, as if it were the Sanhedrin who are on trial for their lives, not himself. He behaves more like a prosecuting attorney than a lawyer for his own defense! His indictment of his hearers has two parts that correspond to the two charges they are bringing against him.

First, Stephen points out that the temple that Solomon built in Jerusalem is merely one chapter in the long history of God's dwelling with his people. God can be present with his people with or without the temple. That is the purpose of his rather lengthy rehearsal of Israel's history. The God of glory appeared to Abraham long before he entered the promised land (Acts 7:2). That same God was with Joseph in Egypt (7:9) and with Moses in Midian (7:30–32). God spoke to his people in the wilderness of Mount Sinai, a generation before they conquered the land. God didn't need a temple in those days to speak to his people. At God's command the tabernacle became the place where the glory of God was made manifest in the midst of his people (Ex. 40:34–35). This tabernacle remained the form of dwelling God had with his people all the way down to the time of David and Solomon, when the temple was finally built (Acts 7:47). Yet even the temple of Solomon was not really God's house; God doesn't dwell in houses that are made with human hands, as Solomon himself confessed at the time (2 Chron. 2:6), and God remained with the remnant of his people even when they were sent into exile in Babylon (Ezek. 11:16). In other words, throughout the Old Testament, the temple was only a symbol of God's presence in the midst of his people, not

1 This is a paraphrase of Spurgeon's words. Spurgeon himself used the image in several sermons. See, for example, C. H. Spurgeon, "The Lover of God's Law Filled with Peace," in *The Metropolitan Tabernacle Pulpit Sermons*, vol. 34 (London: Passmore & Alabaster, 1888), 37.

the reality itself. God's glory could be present with his people with or without a temple.

Second, Stephen makes the point that God's own people have a long history of rejecting the redeemers that he provided for them. This pattern goes all the way back to Joseph, who was rejected by his brothers out of jealousy, yet God used him to deliver them (Acts 7:9–16). The same thing happened to Moses: though God sent him as ruler and redeemer, he was rejected by his own people (7:35). Even after God gave the law through Moses on Mount Sinai, the fathers still refused to obey him, returning in their hearts to Egypt (7:39). Instead of following God's living oracles, they made for themselves a golden calf, a pattern of rebellion that eventually led to the exile from the land God had given them (7:41–43).

It is precisely this pattern of behavior that Stephen's hearers have been continuing—a history of stiff-necked refusal to listen to God. They are continuing in the same attitude that led to the persecution of all the prophets (7:52). This pattern of persecuting the righteous culminated in the killing of "the Righteous One," the supreme prophet like Moses, Jesus, whom Moses himself had prophesied (7:52). In fact, Stephen says, "I'm not the one who has shown disrespect to Moses, to the law, or to the temple—you are!" Crucifying Jesus was the ultimate disrespect to Moses, for he is the one to whom Moses looked forward. Jesus is the ultimate and transcendent prophet like Moses, anticipated in Deuteronomy 18:15.

Crucifying Jesus was also the ultimate disrespect to the law of Moses, for Jesus is the Righteous One, the only one ever to have kept Moses's law fully (Acts 7:52–53). Crucifying Jesus was the ultimate disrespect to the temple, for Jesus is the one to whom the temple looked forward. His body was truly the place where the glory of God was supremely revealed on earth. That is why the apostle John could say, "We have seen his glory, glory as of the only Son from the Father" (John 1:14). That is why Jesus himself said in John 2:19, "Destroy this temple, and in three days I will raise it up." He wasn't talking about reconstituting the physical building in Jerusalem; he was talking about the raising of his own body (John 2:21), which was the manifestation of God's glory in their midst.

Here is Stephen's challenge to his hearers: "I have not shown disrespect to Moses, or to the law, or to the temple: You are the ones guilty of that!"

Putting the Judges on Trial

Stephen thus turns the tables on the Sanhedrin. They are no longer the judges, the people deciding Stephen's case. Now they are the ones on trial, plainly convicted for crucifying Jesus (Acts 7:52). No wonder they were so enraged (7:54)! But if the Sanhedrin is now on trial, the Judge before whom they stand is God himself. That is why the knockout blow is Stephen's vision of heaven opened. What Stephen sees as he dies is nothing less than a glimpse into the heavenly courtroom, a place where the glory of God is present and the resurrected Jesus himself is standing at God's right hand as a witness ready to add his own approval to Stephen's speech (7:55–56). It is the heavenly confirmation of Stephen's condemnation speech, a visual embodiment of the courtroom scene in the book of Daniel, where the Son of Man appears before the Ancient of Days and receives his final vindication on behalf of the saints (Dan. 7:13–14). No wonder the Sanhedrin doesn't want to hear any more of this: it speaks all too clearly of their own condemnation by the God whom they claim to serve (Acts 7:57). So the murderous tradition of the past continues in Stephen's day: having killed the prophets who told ahead of time of the coming of Christ, and having crucified the Righteous One himself, they now stone to death the one who witnessed faithfully to him (7:58).

To the Ends of the Earth

Stephen's speech is a turning point in the book of Acts. Up to this point in the story, we have been in phase one of the expansion of the gospel: The gospel is being proclaimed "in Jerusalem and in all Judea" (Acts 1:8). The gospel is going out to the Jews first, according to God's plan (Rom. 1:16).

In the next chapter, after Stephen's martyrdom, we move on to phase two of the plan: the gospel goes to Samaria, to the despised "half-breeds" (or so the Jews viewed them) who replaced the inhabitants of the former northern kingdom. From there, the gospel proceeds outward to the ends of the earth, just as Jesus declared: "You will be my witnesses in Jerusalem and in all Judea and Samaria, and to the end of the earth" (Acts 1:8).

What triggers the move from phase one to phase two is this definitive rejection of the message of Jesus by the Jewish leaders. As John put it in his gospel, Jesus "came to his own, and his own people did not receive him" (John 1:11).

This Jewish opposition to the gospel is a repeated pattern in the book of Acts. In each place, the message of Jesus is preached first to the Jews, but when they reject it—as they do repeatedly—the gospel messengers then take the good news out to the Gentiles (Acts 18:5–6). It is the hardness of heart on the part of God's own people that provides the open door for the gospel to come to those who by nature are not God's people, to those who are aliens and strangers to God's promises (Rom. 11:25–26). Stephen's death opens the doorway to life to those who up until now have been outsiders to grace. Neither Jews nor Gentiles can come to God through the pathway of Moses, of the law delivered through Moses, or of the temple built by Solomon. Those things have served their purpose, but their time is finished. Jesus, and Jesus alone, is now the pathway to eternal life.

Learning from Stephen's Speech

The lengthy story of Stephen and his speech and stoning hold some important lessons for us.

First, we need to recognize that past religious history is no guide to God's future activity. God is not bound by his past blessings to continue to work in the hearts and lives of a particular people. Sometimes, people talk of America as "a Christian country" as if that label provides some kind of guarantee that it will always be the case. But God's future blessing is in no way guaranteed by his past goodness. God has no grandchildren.

If God could judge his own covenant people, the Jews, as a means of bringing the good news instead to pagan Gentiles, why should he not also at some point judge Americans—and bring into his kingdom instead many from Asia or Africa or South America (see Rom. 11:17–22)? Americans have certainly given him plenty of cause to do so: Americans as a people have become willfully blind and deaf to the gospel. This should cause all Christians to pray earnestly that God would continue to pour out his Holy Spirit in whatever nation we live in, to open the eyes of the spiritually blind and unstop the ears of the spiritually deaf, so that we might see people brought to repentance and faith and the church revived in our time and place. Otherwise, we too could end up just like the Sanhedrin, persecuting God's people in the name of God.

Second, we are not the ones who judge the gospel; it judges us. When we talk to people about God, sometimes we and they both proceed as if they were conducting interviews for the open position of "deity in their life." On our part, we proceed rather apologetically, seeking to persuade people that it is perhaps worth their while to "try Jesus" and see how he does in steering the course of their lives. If all else fails, why not let Jesus take the wheel? People who are not Christians are often very suspicious of such an approach. Who are you to suggest to them which deity they should worship? "Jesus's religion may work for you," they respond, "but I don't have an opening for a deity right now. I'll let you know if a position ever opens up." They speak more truly than they know, for the throne of our hearts is never really vacant. If the living God is not at the center of their lives, something else will surely fill that place, whether they acknowledge it or not.

Stephen's approach to witnessing for Christ is radically different from ours. He doesn't allow his hearers to put themselves in the position of judge: Instead he shows how God's standard has judged them and found them wanting. Even though they knew on some level who God is, they have been stubborn and hard-hearted in resisting him, just like their forefathers before them. The proof of this is seen in the fact that they themselves don't keep God's law that they speak so much about; on the contrary, they have crucified Christ, the only Righteous

One (Acts 7:52–53). But just as God's righteous standard condemns them, so it also condemns each one of us. We have all sinned and fallen short of God's glory (Rom. 3:23). We may not have personally crucified Jesus as they did, but none of us has lived up to God's perfect standard.

Indeed, perhaps our most profound sin lies not so much in the varied ways in which we individually break God's law but in our more fundamental rejection of God's law as having the right to determine our behavior. In other words, our problem isn't simply that we fail to do the things God's law demands. It is that we set ourselves up as the ones who have the right to decide whether God's law is good and deserves to be obeyed or not. Our various outward sins each flow from that inner reality of choosing for ourselves whom we will serve and how we will serve. In reality, however, none of us comes before God positioned as the judge of whether he meets our expectations and aspirations; rather, we stand before him as those who are judged by him and found wanting.

Third, the basis of God's ultimate judgment on you is not your personal morality and spiritual achievements. It is your attitude to Christ and those who bring you the message of Christ. The message of the gospel is always a divisive message because it begins by showing the utter hopelessness of any other method of salvation. That is why the prophets of the Old Testament were persecuted in their day: They denounced the people for their sin and failure, and they announced beforehand the message of the gospel. They foreshadowed the coming of the Righteous One, who would suffer and die in the place of his people. That is why Stephen's hearers crucified Jesus: they couldn't stand his claim to be the Righteous One, the only hope of humanity. That is why they stoned Stephen for daring to proclaim that Jesus was exalted to the Father's right hand as Judge and Savior of the whole world. Jesus put it like this in Luke 10:16: "The one who hears you hears me, and the one who rejects you rejects me, and the one who rejects me rejects him who sent me."

Accepting Jesus Versus Religious Activity

How do you respond when you hear the news that God's holy law convicts you rather than affirms you? God's law demonstrates the fact that you are a sinner who daily falls short of God's perfect standard, and that your only hope of being accepted by God is through the righteousness of Christ being given to you as a free gift. Some have open ears that respond with gratitude and faith: They trust their whole future to this message. Others respond with deaf ears and blind eyes. With a stiff neck and stubborn heart they refuse Jesus Christ, the one whom God sent to be their ruler and Redeemer. The response of faith in Jesus is the only way to life; the response of resistance to this message is the way to spiritual death. There is no middle ground; the gospel always divides.

Religious activity and moral behavior are no substitute for faith in Christ. Many people around us rely on their own goodness—their ability to be decent, upstanding citizens—as their ticket into God's presence. Their trust is essentially in the law and not in Jesus. It may be a trust in a heavy law, a law that binds their behavior in intensely restrictive ways. Or it may be a trust in a very light law, a law that essentially allows them to do whatever they want so long as they can persuade themselves that they mean well. It may even be God's perfect law given through Moses that they are endeavoring to keep to the utmost of their power. Either way, if they are trusting in their own best efforts, they are relying on a law for salvation, and there is no salvation to be found there.

Others trust in their own religious acts—going to church, reading the Bible, avoiding certain obvious sins—as their means of getting to heaven. This is similar to the Jews of Stephen's day who were relying on the temple. "So long as we do the right religious things, we will surely be good with God," they say. Sometimes people combine the two trusts: religious activity often unites people in keeping certain rules because many religions have a basic agreement about what good behavior looks like. But notice that Stephen doesn't condemn his hearers because of their lack of religious activity or because they weren't decent, moral people. These were the Jewish authorities, the religious leaders of their community. They were upstanding citizens, the most religious of their people. They did many of the things the Bible told them to do. But none of that activity would avail them anything before God.

Before God, the very best of us stands exposed as a divine lawbreaker. We all have not only broken God's law but set ourselves up in God's place as the arbiters of right and wrong. God's law lays down the perfect standard of holiness, and we all have rejected that standard and lived deeply flawed lives. We are in desperate need of a righteousness that is not our own, a perfect righteousness that comes to us from the outside. Stephen himself needed the righteousness of another. Only Christ can provide us such righteousness. What we need in our dying moments, when we ourselves must appear before God's judgment seat, is not our best righteousness, flawed and dented as it is. Stephen was not emboldened in his last moments by thoughts of his own faithfulness to God; he didn't see *himself* sitting at God's right hand. What we need is to see at that moment of death is what Stephen saw: Jesus Christ standing at the right hand of the Father for us, ready to welcome us in, testifying on our behalf that his righteousness has been credited to our account. We need to hear words of welcome from God, words that declare to us that we are free from condemnation because we are in Christ and covered by his righteousness.

Confidence in Death

It is that confidence that gave Stephen the ability to die in such a striking way. On the one hand, it was a very brutal death: angry men hurled hard stones, mangling his corpse until his life was gone.

Nonetheless, it was also a beautiful and peaceful death. His last words are words of grace and forgiveness, unmistakably echoing the words of Jesus on the cross: "Lord Jesus, receive my spirit. . . . Lord, do not hold this sin against them" (Acts 7:59–60; see Luke 23:34, 46). Notice too the very last words of the chapter: "When he had said this, he fell asleep" (Acts 7:60). What an astonishing description of such a death! We might easily use that metaphor of someone passing away peacefully at home, but here? Yes! In the midst of the brutality and pain of a martyr's death, Stephen had such peace and confidence in God that he gave up his life as easily as if he were simply taking a nap.

How was Stephen able to die in such a terrible way with such incredible peace, when you and I often struggle even to live through an ordinary day with peace? I don't need to face an angry mob holding stones to feel anxious. My fears can be stirred simply by feeling unprepared for a class I have to give or by facing up to a person I have to confront over their sin. Many of us are likewise paralyzed by worry over our health or our future at work or our marriages and families or because we don't feel that we are as far on in life as others who are our age. We don't have the same peace that Stephen had.

Clearly, Stephen's peace was a remarkable gift of God, given to him for precisely this eventuality—so we don't need to beat ourselves up because we can't measure up to Stephen. What God gave him in that moment was simply this: Stephen was enabled to fix his eyes firmly on Christ, to know that the real Judge before whom he had to give an account would not condemn him but welcome him. We are constantly fearful because we forget these things. When we forget the gospel verdict on us, we hand the authority to judge us over to other human beings and to life circumstances. If people praise us and circumstances work out the way we want, then we believe we are wonderful human beings. If people criticize us and our lives aren't going according to plan, then we are devastated. When our remaining sin flares up and we are exposed to others as unholy—as still rank, lawbreaking sinners—we are crushed. But these idols are not our judge. They may have the power to fire us from our jobs, to play havoc with our emotions, to abandon us and let us down, to burden us with guilt. These idols may even have the power to kill us. But they do not have the power to judge our lives and deliver a final verdict on our identity and our destiny. That power rests in the hands of our heavenly Father and in his hands alone.

Will my heavenly Father agree with my earthly judges and discard me? If I am no Stephen, boldly trusting in God and proclaiming Jesus in the face of death, will I be turned away? By no means! Our Judge is the same heavenly Father who sent his own Son to die a far more terrible death than any human court could ever decree. At his right hand in that heavenly courtroom stands that same Son, holding out his wounded hands, the hands that have the nail prints still in them—not just any nail prints, but *my* nail prints—the prints of nails that have my sins written all over them. Yet at any moment of my life if I could only see into heaven as Stephen did, I would see the same thing that he saw: the Son of Man standing at the right hand of the Father, welcoming me into the Father's presence through his own perfect obedience.

Puritan-era pastor Samuel Rutherford knew the same kind of suffering and persecution that we see in Acts. The authorities ejected him from his ministry in the southwest of Scotland when he wrote in defense of the doctrines of grace. They sent him to Aberdeen in northeast Scotland, a cold and dreary place to live at the best of times. Much later in his life, after Charles II came to the throne, Rutherford faced charges of treason for arguing in *Lex Rex* that monarchs were not above the law. He replied to his court summons from his deathbed: "Tell them I have got a summons already before a superior Judge and judicatory, and I behove to answer my first summons, and ere your day come I will be where few kings and great folks come."[2] Rutherford knew that his Redeemer was pleading his case and that he would surely be heard by the great Judge.

To the extent that God enables us to grasp that truth and fix our eyes on the risen and exalted Jesus, then we will be ready not merely to die like Stephen but to live like him. In death as in life, Stephen was a picture of peace and grace, of faith and sure hope. He knew there was no condemnation in heaven for him, and that knowledge fitted him for both life and death. If we grasp that same gospel, then whatever sticks and stones the world can muster against us, we will have an enduring peace far beyond anything the world can give, or take away, or even understand, safely encompassed by the grace of God.

2 Cited in Joel R. Beeke and Randall J. Pederson, *Meet the Puritans: With a Guide to Modern Reprints* (Reformation Heritage Books, 2006), 727.

12

The Gospel Spreads

Acts 8:1–25

IN JANUARY, 1956, five young American missionaries, Jim Elliot, Nate Saint, Roger Youderian, Pete Fleming, and Ed McCully were brutally speared to death by members of the Waodani tribe, with whom they had sought to share the gospel.[1] Remarkably, a mere two years later, Rachel Saint (Nate's sister) and Elisabeth Elliot (Jim's widow), along with her young daughter, Valerie, returned to Ecuador. There they brought the gospel to the same Waodani tribe, seeing many converted to Christ, including some of those who took part in the original massacre. The gospel overrode a multitude of reasons for hating and fearing one another, bringing love and fellowship where once there had been hatred and division.

In a similar way, there was a long history of profound enmity between the Jews and the Samaritans that should have made it intensely hard for the new Christians, who mostly came from a Jewish background, to imagine the gospel going to their most hated enemies. Yet in the book of Acts, we see those deep and enduring divisions being bridged as the gospel goes out from Jerusalem to Judea and then onward to Samaria and finally to the Gentiles—to us!

1 The story is recounted in Elisabeth Elliot, *Through Gates of Splendor* (Harper & Brothers, 1957).

At each key transition point in his narrative, Luke is careful to document the first incursion of the gospel into new territory. Each time, it is accompanied with a fresh outpouring of the Holy Spirit to authenticate its validity in the face of opponents of the gospel who insist that any outsider who becomes a Christian first has to become a Jew and live according to all the requirements of the Mosaic covenant—eating only kosher food, observing feasts, and so on. On the contrary, Luke repeatedly stresses the fact that when outsiders become Christians, no burdens are placed upon them apart from simple faith in Christ. The gospel is freely distributed to all the world as the Spirit brings men and women from every tribe and nation to faith in Christ.

In this passage, we see that though God's own people decisively reject the gospel, stoning to death its messengers as they did to the prophets before them, that rejection itself becomes the means by which the gospel reaches a wider—and eager—audience. God is at work even through suffering and persecution to accomplish his redemptive purposes. The gospel now comes freely to all people regardless of their race, nationality, or religious background.

This was, of course, God's purpose from the beginning, as the promise in the book of Genesis that all nations would find a blessing for themselves in Abraham's offspring showed (Gen. 12:1–3). But now that purpose finds its fruition through the ascension of Jesus into heaven and the outpouring of his Holy Spirit, not only on Jews and their children but on those who are far off as well (Acts 2:39).

Increasing Persecution Spreads the Gospel

The passage opens with the news of a great persecution of the church in Jerusalem that follows the stoning of Stephen, the first Christian martyr (Acts 8:1). It seems that this persecution particularly focuses on the Hellenistic Christians; it's almost as if, by electing seven Hellenistic deacons to oversee the food distribution ministry, the early church has unwittingly painted a target on the backs of this part of the Christian community. Following Stephen's death, Philip—another of the seven protodeacons (6:5)—becomes an obvious next victim, so he leaves town along with many other early Christians. The apostles themselves don't seem to be directly affected in this assault on the early church; perhaps their Jewish status gives them a measure of protection. But many ordinary Christians, along with leaders like Philip, conclude that it's time to pack their bags and go out to find new homes in Judea or even in Samaria.

These Christians don't leave Jerusalem in orderly fashion. Luke tells us they are "scattered" (Acts 8:4), which is a theologically loaded word in the light of Israel's history of exile.[2] They become part of the diaspora—the scattered people of God (Isa. 11:12). But whereas in the past God's scattering of his people has been the result of their sin, a punishment to be endured, now it is the means whereby the good news of life through Jesus Christ comes to many people who would never have traveled to encounter it in Jerusalem. The pattern of ministry in the Old Testament was that Israel was supposed to be a light to the nations, drawing them on a pilgrimage to meet their God in Jerusalem (Isa. 49:6). This pattern is now reversed, so that the church is sent out as a light in a dark world to bring the gospel to the nations (Matt. 5:14). No longer will the nations need to travel to Jerusalem to worship; now, through Jesus Christ, they can worship in the true heavenly temple that is above (Heb. 12:22–24).

This, not coincidentally, was the topic of an earlier conversation between Jesus and a Samaritan woman beside a well at Sychar (John 4:4–7). The woman sought to divert attention from her own dubious moral condition, so she asked Jesus whether worship should properly be offered on Mount Gerizim (where the Samaritans worshiped and had had their own temple until the Hasmonean Jewish leader John Hyrcanus destroyed it in around 111 BC) or whether they should travel to worship with the Jews in Jerusalem (John 4:20). The right answer to that question was not in debate in the period of the Old Testament:

2 The same word is used in the Septuagint of Isaiah 56:8, where God speaks of gathering eunuchs and foreigners to himself alongside the "scattered of Israel" (author's translation). Not coincidentally, later in Acts 8, the scattering of the new Israel, the church, leads to the inclusion of an Ethiopian eunuch in God's people.

worship could only properly be offered in Jerusalem. That was the place where God had chosen to place his name—and particularly in the temple Solomon built (1 Kings 8:16–20). The centralization of worship in Jerusalem was a key measure of the faithfulness of Old Testament kings. This was probably part of Hyrcanus's motivation in destroying the Gerizim temple. But, remarkably, Jesus told the Samaritan woman that in the future worship would no longer be offered either in Jerusalem or on Mount Gerizim but rather "in Spirit and truth" (John 4:21–23). With Jesus's coming, a profound transition had taken place in redemptive history: now, in Jesus himself, the presence of God that hitherto had resided in the Jerusalem temple had taken flesh and walked among them. He was himself the new temple (John 2:19). Now worship would no longer be offered simply in Jerusalem but wherever two or three were gathered in Jesus's name (Matt. 18:20).

This is the reality that is beginning to be enacted at this point in the book of Acts. Up until this point, Jerusalem has still been the center of the religious universe. Jesus's crucifixion, resurrection, and ascension all took place near Jerusalem, and Jesus told the apostles to wait in Jerusalem until they received power from on high. This did in fact happen on the day of Pentecost. Since then Luke has shown us the explosive growth of the new church in Jerusalem. At this point, the temple was itself still a base for the teaching ministry of the apostles. But that situation was never intended to last. The gospel was to go out from Jerusalem, to search out true worshipers wherever they were, including the Samaritan woman and now many of her compatriots (Acts 1:8).

Although this expansion was always God's purpose for the gospel, it is interesting that the trigger for this movement was not a successful missions conference or the report of a study committee in the Jerusalem church. Rather, it was the result of a fierce persecution that engulfed the early believers and drove many of them out, sharing the good news as they went. Some commentators think that there is an implicit critique of the apostles here—for staying in Jerusalem rather than spreading out to fulfill the Great Commission after the Spirit came. I understand that argument, but I'm not persuaded. There seems no reluctance on the part of Peter and John to go down to Samaria once they are invited to visit the new work there. Rather, I think the apostles' initial focus on Jerusalem is more likely to be the natural consequence of the success of the early church in reaching those immediately around them. The apostles are probably run ragged trying to shepherd and oversee the church in Jerusalem, having no time to think more widely about the larger task with which they have been entrusted.

But God's program of world mission is not hindered by their preoccupation. He uses whatever means are necessary to get the good news out, even persecution. Often, we view negative circumstances like persecution as something to pray against and ask God for protection from. It is certainly reasonable that we should pray like this. Yet we should also remember that God will use precisely such negative circumstances in our own lives just as he did in the lives of the early church—in order to accomplish his good purposes in us as well as through us. What looks to us like a personal disaster may actually be God opening a new door to ministry.

The Role of Saul

A leading activist in this persecution of the early church is a man named Saul, whom we will later know better as Paul (Acts 8:3). He was a student of the famous Pharisee Gamaliel, the man who earlier urged the Jewish leaders to leave the early Christians to sink or swim without interference (5:34–39).

But Saul does not follow his teacher when it comes to how to react to the new Christian movement. He sees it as a dangerous heresy, and he seeks to suppress it by every means possible.

Ironically, the means Saul uses to suppress the church are the very means God uses to grow the church. What Saul means for evil, God means for good (see Gen. 50:20). He is simply pouring gasoline on the fire: Wherever the displaced early Christians go, they also preach the gospel, bringing it to multiple new locations in a very short time.

That in itself is striking. If I were to be persecuted and forced out of my home for my faith in Christ, I think I would try to hide my identity.

I'd downplay the whole Christianity thing, at least for a while, hoping to remain safe.

But the early Christians are very different. Wherever they go, they "gossip" the good news. Some of them are formally appointed preachers like Philip, but many of them must be ordinary laypeople who simply respond to the natural questions about the reasons for their relocation by telling people about Jesus. In one respect these people have an obvious open door—when people ask, "So, why did you move to Samaria?" they just asked to hear the gospel, since the gospel is the reason for the move.

I suspect that many of us today, if we found ourselves in that situation, would mumble something generic about better job prospects, or a better future for our children, something that might be partially true and that can't come back to haunt us.

Kingdom-Focused Living

This ministry is all the more surprising because normally Jews and Samaritans did not interact at all. Jews would often take the long way around if they had to travel from Galilee to Jerusalem. They did this specifically in order to avoid passing through Samaria. Samaritans felt similarly, especially since it was only around a hundred years since the Jews had invaded their land and destroyed their temple.

So it is remarkable that those Christians who are scattered go to live not only in Judea or Galilee but in Samaria as well. The only explanation for such a radical choice is that they remember Jesus's words about the gospel going to Samaria, and they overcome their natural prejudices in support of the mission that Jesus has assigned to the church. In the same way that some in the early church sell houses and lands to support the spread of the good news (Acts 4:34–37), others respond to the loss of their property by moving somewhere where the gospel has not been preached, to enhance the work in that place.

This kingdom focus should be very challenging to us. We often evaluate our options in life on the basis of our own interests. We want to live somewhere pleasant, safe, and comfortable. We want jobs and ministry positions that pay well, utilize our gifts, and support our families. None of these things are wrong in themselves. But we should also be asking kingdom questions: Where has the gospel not been preached? Is God calling me to be part of this work even though it will be a tough assignment? We need to be careful here: a need does not constitute a call. We are not simply to look for the hardest possible posting for ourselves and our families and assume that God is necessarily calling us to do that. But we should be open to God calling us to a difficult work that moves us far outside our comfort zone for the sake of the gospel. In particular, we should be open to consider that God might call us outside our normal context of race, ethnicity, and social class for the sake of the gospel. The spread of God's kingdom deserves nothing less.

The Samaritan Pentecost

Philip is among those who are displaced (Acts 8:5). He goes to a city in Samaria—perhaps the city of Samaria itself or, more likely, some other town in that region such as Sychar or Shechem. There Philip replicates the activity of the apostles in Jerusalem, casting out unclean spirits, healing the lame and the crippled, and preaching the gospel as he goes (8:5–7; cf. Acts 3). More precisely, the text says he proclaims the Messiah to them (8:5) while also casting out unclean spirits and healing people (8:6). The signs and wonders that he performs are secondary to the message; they support and authenticate Philip as the messenger of God himself. But their primary function is to support the message about Jesus, not to be the message. The result of this powerful message is great joy in the city, as the people "with one accord" (Greek: *homothumadon*) pay attention to the ministry of Philip (8:6). There is a contrast here that is a bit more visible in the Greek, for Luke just used that same word to refer to the Sanhedrin who screamed out and "together" (*homothumadon*) rushed to attack Stephen (7:57). The Jews single-mindedly refuse their Messiah and kill his messenger; the despised Samaritans single-mindedly receive the message about Jesus with great joy! They believe in the name of Jesus and are eagerly baptized into God's people (8:12). Just as God foretold in the Old Testament, the outsiders are much more eager to believe than God's own people.

The Samaritans do not immediately receive the Holy Spirit upon becoming Christians, however. This is not because the Samaritans are second-class citizens of the kingdom of God or need to wait for a second blessing in order to become a full part of the church. Indeed, it is for exactly the opposite reason that they do not receive the Spirit (until after a short delay). There must be no question that the Samaritans have been fully included in the people of God, and for that reason, it is important that the apostles be involved in the process. Peter and John need to see with their own eyes this important step forward in redemptive history, and the Samaritans need to be welcomed in by the apostles themselves—so there can be no question later that they, too, have been included in the one people of God.

So when the apostles hear about this staggering development, no less than Peter and John come down to see with their own eyes what is happening (8:14). This is the same John who, with his brother James, had been eager in the Gospels to call down fire from heaven on a Samaritan village that refused to receive Jesus (Luke 9:54). But when they see what is going on in Samaria, they pray for the Samaritans that they might receive a different kind of fire from heaven—the Pentecostal fire that represents the pouring out of the Holy Spirit (Acts 8:15; cf. 2:3). In response to their prayers, the Holy Spirit is poured out with power on the Samaritans too (8:17). No one can doubt that they have moved from death to life in Jesus and have been added to the kingdom.

Not for Sale

Interspersed with this joyful story of the conversion even of the Samaritans and their inclusion in God's people, however, there is the tragic story of Simon Magus, or Simon the magician. Just as the story of Ananias and Sapphira soberingly interrupts the story of the Jerusalem church's early growth (Acts 5:1–11), so Simon's story adds a warning note to the coming of the gospel to Samaria. Simon is already a well-known celebrity in Samaria as the story begins. He is accustomed to amazing the inhabitants with his own brand of dramatic signs and wonders (8:9). He claims to be someone great—"the power of God that is called Great," a claim that has messianic or semidivine overtones (8:10). Yet even he is amazed by the powerful ministry of Philip. We are told that he "believed" in Jesus. He is even baptized into the name of Jesus as part of this new church. As one who deals in power, Simon is naturally fascinated with the greater power that Philip possesses, and he follows him around everywhere. He is even more astounded when Peter and John lay hands on the new believers and the Holy Spirit descends upon them. All Simon can see, however, are the commercial possibilities of such power; he is willing to pay whatever initiation fee is necessary to receive that power and be able to pass it on to others (for a suitable fee).

In some respects, Simon's response is the opposite response to that of the Jews. They want to stamp out the gospel through persecution; Simon wants to spread the gospel by franchising it. But such efforts would be just as destructive as the Jews' persecution. There have been many throughout the history of the church who have similarly sought to profit through offering a perversion of the gospel, whether in the form of the Roman Catholic practice of selling indulgences—one of the causes of the Reformation, and a practice that continues today—or in the form of the health and wealth preachers, who promise God's blessings in return for substantial donations to their ministries. But if it is for sale, it isn't the gospel. The gospel always comes to us freely. The cost of our salvation has been entirely borne for us by Christ; there is nothing left for us to contribute. Even our required faith in Christ is a free gift from God himself.

As a result, we can see that even though Simon professes faith in Christ and has been baptized, his heart is not right with God. He is not really trusting in Christ, or he would never have made such a request of Peter. You might expect Simon to be instantly struck down for his presumption, as Ananias and Sapphira were before him (see Acts 5:5, 10). Surely his sin is far greater than theirs! Yet Peter graciously confronts Simon with the reality of his need for repentance and forgiveness (8:20–23). Even now the door is open to Simon to confess his sin and turn and be healed. We're not told explicitly in the book of Acts whether Simon repents. Simon simply asks Peter to pray for him that the curse he pronounced on his silver should not come into effect (8:24).

That's not a promising response; it's not really repentance to pray that the judgment you deserve will be suspended. True repentance acknowledges your sins and prays that they would be forgiven and that God might give you a new heart that desires to change. Indeed, the early church records Simon Magus among the early gnostic heretics who sought to pervert the gospel and turn it into the means for personal gain, which would have been entirely in character.[3]

God's Sovereignty in Salvation

So what do we learn from these stories of the Samaritans and of Simon Magus? The first and most obvious lesson is that in order to make clear God's utter sovereignty in salvation sometimes the gospel goes to outsiders and outcasts—especially when insiders and "likely believers" reject it. The Jews who knew the Scriptures from birth refused to listen to God's accredited messengers just as they had refused to listen to Jesus. They persecuted the church, stoning Stephen for his bold proclamation of the gospel (Acts 7). But the Samaritans, who were on no one's list of fertile soil for the gospel, responded to its message with eagerness and joy. The Jews had the entire Old Testament—the Law, the Prophets, and the Psalms—and its pages spoke of the sufferings of Christ and the glories that would follow (Luke 24:44). Yet though they knew the Scriptures many of them missed the Jesus of whom those Scriptures spoke. The Samaritans had nothing but a slightly garbled version of the Pentateuch, with some key texts altered and adapted. But the Spirit brought many of them to joyful faith in Christ. The hardest nut in this entire chapter, Saul himself, would eventually be converted by this same gospel (see Acts 9).

This story should encourage us to be bold in our witness to the most unlikely of people. Some of our friends and family members seem un-

3 David G. Peterson, *The Acts of the Apostles*, Pillar New Testament Commentary (Eerdmans, 2009), 282.

likely prospective converts. I think of a relative of mine in England who chose to get married in a Unitarian Universalist church. The entire service was a blatant denial of the existence and goodness of God. During it the pastor explicitly mocked the resurrection. I love my relative, who is a larger-than-life character, but he's someone I struggle to imagine coming to faith in Christ. Increasingly, though, he is representative of the religious thoughts and views of my fellow countrymen, who have thrown off even a routine, formal nod in a religious direction at such moments. Yet are my post-Christian fellow Brits a harder nut to crack than the Samaritans, or is my relative more opposed to God than Saul? The gospel has the power to transform his heart too.

The reality is that everyone who has not trusted in Christ is dead in their transgressions and sins (Eph. 2:1). That means that people who may seem to have everything that ought to make them open and friendly to the gospel still need nothing less than a miraculous intervention of God to bring them to faith in Christ, while the person on the planet who is most opposed to the gospel needs no greater intervention than that. So we should pray persistently and earnestly for all those whom we meet who are without Christ, and we should be bold in seeking to bring the good news even to those who—humanly speaking—seem far from grace.

Baptized Unbelievers

At the same time, this passage reminds us that it is possible for people to have a profession of faith and even be baptized (as an adult!) and not really be a believer. That is a sobering truth. Sometimes we are too eager to latch onto the first profession of faith that people make, as if saying particular words prove beyond doubt that this person is surely a believer. In reality, conversion is a mysterious thing. Sometimes people may have genuine faith that is very small and takes a long time to grow into anything recognizable. At other times, as Jesus pointed out in the parable of the soils, they may have an apparent faith that springs up quickly, like seeds germinating in shallow soil, but dies away equally rapidly in the face of difficulties (Matt. 13:3–9).

What should we do with that reality? I don't think we are called to have a deep suspicion of every profession of faith so that we are not ready to encourage anyone to have assurance of salvation before they are at least eighty years old and are living an utterly blameless life. But neither should we naively assume that every profession of faith is genuine. It's not always necessary (or even possible) for us to sort out the true from the false profession, as Jesus himself noted in the parable of the wheat and the weeds (Matt. 13:23–30). We do our best to ascertain a credible profession of faith before we admit someone to membership of the church and to the Lord's Table. But we should be neither overly cynical nor overly naive in that assessment. We can be charitable and take someone at their word that they are trusting in Christ, while pressing them onward to the kinds of behaviors, attitudes, and actions that flow from a true understanding of Christ and the gospel. Meanwhile, there may be times in the exercise of church discipline where we are called on to make the solemn judgment that someone's behavior and expressed attitudes make their profession of faith in Christ "incredible," and to warn them that repentance and forgiveness are necessary for all who are genuinely part of the kingdom of God and who are truly indwelled by the Holy Spirit.

However, the most fundamental application of the stories we just explored in Acts 8 should be a reminder to all of us to search our own individual hearts. Am I genuinely trusting in Christ for my salvation? Am I seeking by God's grace to repent from my sin and turn from it, asking for God's forgiveness on an ongoing basis? Or do I simply say the same words as other people while not really believing them in my heart? Am I in church because of what I think I can get out of it or because this is where I come to hear the gospel week after week?

This is a call to sobering, but not crushing, self-examination. We are all a mixed bag of messed-up motives. That is why the gospel itself constantly calls us to take our eyes off ourselves and fix them on Christ, who is our perfect righteousness. We are saved by believing in Jesus, not by the strength of our faith in Jesus. More precisely, as Jesus himself said to the Samaritan woman, we are saved by the Father who is seeking us, not by our successfully seeking the Father (John 4:23). No one the Father gives the Son will ever be lost (John 6:37–39). God gives us faith as a free gift, unlikely candidates for heaven though we are, with a heart that is often not right before God, tainted by bitterness and bound up in iniquity. We are certainly no better as people than Simon Magus, but by God's grace we have been brought to recognize that fact and repent of it. We have been brought to look to Christ's righteousness in our place that is sufficient for former magicians, for Samaritans, even for former persecuting Pharisees like Paul—and therefore must surely be sufficient for us.

This reality ought to bring us great and contagious joy! By God's grace we are not what we once were: dead in our sinful attitudes and actions. We are indwelled by the Holy Spirit, whose power gives us the ability to begin to recognize our sins and repent from them, and who has promised to complete the work of sanctifying us on the last day (Phil. 1:6). To be sure, we are not yet what we shall be. But even now we who once were far off have become children of God in Christ, included in God's family. This is good news indeed, to all those to whom the Holy Spirit gives eyes to see. This is a great gospel that we should long to take to the ends of the earth, to the most unlikely of people, that they too might be made children of God.

13

An Open Doorway to God

Acts 8:26–40

WHEN I WAS A BOY, I loved throwing stones into the water. Small, flat stones could be skimmed over the surface, skipping once, twice, even as many as ten or more times if you were skillful enough. Big stones were best tossed in to make a splash. The bigger the stone and the higher the trajectory, the bigger the resulting splash. When you throw a stone into a pond, the ripples spread outward from the point of impact; if you throw in a stone big enough, the ripples spread a long way. Acts 8 opens with the throwing of some big stones, both literally and metaphorically. Literally, some large stones have just been tossed at Stephen, stones aimed at silencing his persistent witness to Christ. His voice was stilled, though not before he witnessed his testimony to having seen the risen Christ one final, dramatic time (7:55–56).

From that one incident, persecution—a great persecution, according to Acts 8:1—spreads to the rest of the Jerusalem church. The goal of this persecution is to silence the Jesus movement once and for all. The end result, however, is simply to spread its influence more widely, as the rest of Acts 8 demonstrates. The ripples indeed spread outward, accomplishing God's purposes along the way.

An Unlikely Convert

The Ethiopian eunuch is one among many individuals who are touched positively by the ripples flowing out from that early persecution. Why is his story in particular preserved for us?

It is not simply because Philip provides a model for us of how to do personal evangelism. Although there are probably many lessons we could learn from him, none of us are apostles, and few of us will find ourselves directed by the angel of the Lord to particular evangelistic encounters (Acts 8:26). None of us get caught up by the Spirit and transported to a new location when we have finished speaking to our friends about Jesus (8:39). There's a much bigger story here than Five Tips for Improving Your Personal Evangelism. In this passage, we see God's grace reaching out to the most unlikely of persons and bringing him into the kingdom—just as the Scriptures had foretold in the book of Isaiah. God is the truly effective evangelist in this passage, not Philip.

To begin with, we need to see that this passage shows us an unlikely convert in the Ethiopian eunuch. By nature, he is a doubly disadvantaged outsider. He is a foreigner, an Ethiopian, a black African from a faraway land. He was not born into the covenant community. He was not even born into the "half-breed" Samaritans, as the Jews viewed them. These mixed descendants of the northern kingdom at least had some traditional understanding of the God of the Scriptures (2 Kings 17:24). The man to whom God sends Philip is a complete outsider by birth.

The Ethiopian is also an outsider by life situation. He is a eunuch. He was deliberately physically deformed, probably at an early age, as were many government officials in the ancient world. In fact, so common was the overlap between eunuch and government official that the same Hebrew word, *saris*, is used for both. As a eunuch, a person could serve the royal family without being considered a threat to the women in the royal household or a potential rival to the king. Career wise, being a eunuch was a significant advantage in the civil service. Socially, it was perfectly acceptable. Some eunuchs even got married. But think of the psychological damage they must have suffered. Religiously, as far as the covenant community was concerned, it was a catastrophe. In Deuteronomy 23:1, all eunuchs were permanently excluded from the assembly of God's people. Their condition was a breach of God's order in creation, in which he created two sexes, male and female, not three. His deficiency was emblematic of the deficiencies and shortcomings of sin: only the pure, the whole, and the complete could enter into the presence of the King of kings.

A Frustrated Outsider

So the Ethiopian eunuch is an outsider by birth and by life situation, yet he nonetheless wants to become part of the covenant community. He wants inclusion badly enough to make the long and arduous journey from Ethiopia to Jerusalem, desiring to worship Israel's God (Acts 8:27). The text doesn't tell us what he experiences when he gets to Jerusalem, perhaps because it is all too predictable. There is a "No entry" sign on the temple door for people like him (see Deut. 23:1). At best, he can watch from a distance while others enter into God's presence in the temple and sing God's praises. This eunuch seems condemned to a life forever on the outside, looking in. He must surely be going away from Jerusalem frustrated by the barriers that exist between him and God.

The Ethiopian eunuch is also frustrated in his attempts to read the Scriptures, as Acts 8 reveals. On his way home from the temple, he seeks fellowship with God by reading God's word, but he finds the Bible obscure and difficult to understand. He reads aloud from the scroll of Isaiah (Acts 8:28), which he has likely purchased at great cost in Jerusalem. But he can't grasp the significance of the passage (8:31). Is the prophet describing his own experience when he speaks of being cut off like a lamb before its slaughterers, or is he describing the experience of someone else, whether another individual or the whole Jewish people (8:34)? He can read the words on the page, but he can't grasp what they are about. It seems as if every doorway into God's presence is utterly closed to him. God might be accessible for other people, but there is surely no hope for him.

Into that situation of darkness and despair, God personally sends a powerful witness to this unlikely convert. Philip is the one who has brought the good news about Jesus to the Samaritans—another unlikely context for effective evangelism (8:5–8). Now the Spirit of God directs Philip on a new mission, a mission that takes him out on the desert road south and west of Jerusalem, the opposite direction from Samaria (8:26–28). There, obedient to the Spirit's leading, Philip overhears the Ethiopian eunuch reading the Scriptures and asks him if he understands what he is reading (8:30). That simple question opens the door for the evangelistic encounter that follows. The Ethiopian invites him up into his chariot and, starting with that very passage of Scripture, Philip tells him about Jesus (8:35). Just like the downcast disciples on the Emmaus road that first Easter Sunday, the Ethiopian has his eyes opened to Jesus Christ, who is the message of the whole of the Bible (Luke 24:25–27). Philip tells him that Jesus is the one of whom the prophet speaks. Jesus, the Lamb of God, is the one who was silent before his judges (Isa. 53:7), the Jewish Sanhedrin. Jesus is the one who was denied earthly justice and whose life was brutally taken away, so that he had no physical descendants (Isa. 53:8).

Though Philip starts with the passage of Scripture that the eunuch is reading, he doesn't stop there. He goes on to unpack the rest of Isaiah 53 for him: Jesus is the one whom the prophet foresees, who is cut off for the transgression of his people (Isa. 53:5). Jesus takes up our infirmities and carries our sorrows on the cross (Isa. 53:4). He is pierced for our transgressions; he is crushed for our iniquities (Isa. 53:5). Even though Jesus has no descendants physically—just like the eunuch—Isaiah 53 says he will see his offspring (Isa. 53:10). Through the gospel, his spiritual descendants would be numerous.

Philip shows the eunuch how the straightforward message of the gospel is at the heart of the Old Testament prophet's message: we have sinned and gone astray like lost sheep, and we deserve to be eternally cut off (Isa. 53:6). Oxen know their owner and donkeys respect their master, but we have all failed to recognize who God is and to give him the respect and obedience he deserves (Isa. 1:3). Dumb beasts have a more accurate perspective on the world than any of us do by nature! Nonetheless, out of God's grace and mercy, he has taken all our iniquities and sins and laid them on Jesus Christ on the cross so that we might become the family of God.

The Gospel Made Personal

The Ethiopian eunuch needs more than the facts of the simple gospel to feed his soul, however. He needs to have the gospel made personal, to know that this gospel is for him too. It's all very well to say that Jesus Christ "died for the sins of his people," that he was "crucified for our transgressions," but does that "our" have room for the total outsider, a eunuch from Ethiopia? The answer to that question is to be found just a few columns further on in his Isaiah scroll:

> For thus says the Lord:
> "To the eunuchs who keep my Sabbaths,
> who choose the things that please me
> and hold fast my covenant,
> I will give in my house and within my walls
> a monument and a name
> better than sons and daughters;
> I will give them an everlasting name
> that shall not be cut off.
>
> "And the foreigners who join themselves to the Lord,
> to minister to him, to love the name of the Lord,
> and to be his servants,
> everyone who keeps the Sabbath and does not profane it,
> and holds fast my covenant—
> these I will bring to my holy mountain,
> and make them joyful in my house of prayer;
> their burnt offerings and their sacrifices
> will be accepted on my altar;

for my house shall be called a house of prayer
for all peoples."
The Lord God,
who gathers the outcasts of Israel, declares,
"I will gather yet others to him
besides those already gathered." (Isa. 56:4–8)

There may have been a "No entry" sign over the temple in Jerusalem for people like the Ethiopian eunuch, but this prophecy in Isaiah speaks of a time when there will be an open door for them, too, into the people of God. The prophet foresees the time when God's house will be a house of prayer for all nations (Isa. 56:7). The prophet knows that along with the scattered Israelites (Acts 8:1), God will also gather many people from many nations—including eunuchs—to be his people (Isa. 56:8; 19:23–25). Even the place where their meeting takes place—the "desert," or "wilderness" (Acts 8:26)—is the place where Isaiah anticipated a voice crying out the coming salvation, so the eunuch's encounter with Philip is a living fulfillment of Isaiah 40:3.[1]

This shift from exclusion to inclusion for the nations and for those with physical impairments is itself the fruit of the work of the suffering servant of Isaiah 53. It is the cutting off of the Perfect One, who bears all our sins and transgressions, that opens the door to all those who are morally crippled and spiritually emasculated to come to God. So Philip declared to the Ethiopian eunuch that what the ancient prophet had foretold had now come about through the gospel. In Christ, there is neither Jew nor Gentile, slave nor free, male nor female, whole or eunuch. All who come to God by faith come on the same terms, with

1 Patrick Schreiner, *Acts*, in Christian Standard Commentary (Holman Reference, 2021), 284. There are other connections with Isaiah in the passage as well. The surprising discovery of water in the wilderness in Acts 8:36 also fulfills the promise of Isaiah 35:6 that when the Lord redeemed his people, water would break forth in the wilderness. Likewise, the Greek word usually translated "south" in Acts 8:26 more often means "at noon," which provides a connection to Isaiah 58:10, "Then shall your light rise in the darkness / and your gloom be as the noonday," speaking of the renewed Israel's impact for blessing on the nations around them.

empty hands, and are now one in Christ (Gal. 3:11). In Christ, there is an open door to God for the eunuch too.

That explains the eunuch's response to Philip's words. He says to Philip, "What *prevents* me from being baptized?" (Acts 8:36). Here is a man whose whole life has been spent on the outside looking in: there was always some fine print that meant that someone like him was not included. But Philip explains to him with great joy that now, finally, there is a door that is open to him too! There is nothing to prevent even someone like him from coming in to the community through baptism. No wonder he goes on his way rejoicing (8:39). The Ethiopian eunuch has found Christ, and in him he has found both joy and understanding—in a new life that would last forever.

Me Too?

Luke isn't interested in merely recounting an encouraging story here. This account demands a response from you, whoever you are—whether you are an outsider to God or an insider. If you are an outsider to God, the story of Philip and the Ethiopian eunuch challenges all the reasons you may have for not coming into the covenant community. Perhaps you think you can't come into God's presence because of your background. Maybe you have never been part of the church, and so you don't feel like you could ever belong; maybe there is some particular sin you have committed that you think must surely bar you forever—adultery, divorce, abortion, murder. Maybe there is some life-dominating sin against which you struggle and constantly fail—alcoholism, same-sex attraction, lust, internet pornography, pride, compulsive shopping. Perhaps you know that there are all kinds of things about your life that seem like they ought to bar the entryway to God to someone like you.

If that is your situation, then the story of the Ethiopian eunuch should give you fresh hope. There was an open door into God's house for this man in spite of his failings and physical deficiencies. In Christ, he was welcome to come in. This is because when anyone comes to God by faith in Christ, he doesn't come by himself trusting in his own worthiness. He or she simply says, "God, please receive me, not for my sake but for Christ's. Don't look at my deficiencies. Don't even look at my good qualities. Look at his blood shed to cover my transgressions. Look at his righteousness, substituted for my best efforts."

Paul puts it like this in 1 Corinthians 6:9–11:

> Or do you not know that the unrighteous will not inherit the kingdom of God? Do not be deceived: neither the sexually immoral, nor idolaters, nor adulterers, nor men who practice homosexuality, nor thieves, nor the greedy, nor drunkards, nor revilers, nor swindlers will inherit the kingdom of God. And such were some of you. But you were washed, you were sanctified, you were justified in the name of the Lord Jesus Christ and by the Spirit of our God.

In Christ, the door to God is wide open to you no matter who you are, no matter what you've done. His blood is sufficient to atone for you too. His righteousness is good enough to sanctify even you. His Spirit will ultimately present even you without spot before God. There is no condemnation for you if you are in Christ. Nothing prevents you from coming to Christ and being welcomed in right now!

Insiders Who Are Really Outsiders

On the other hand, the story of the eunuch should also challenge some people who assume that they are insiders with God. Jerusalem was the place where the Ethiopian eunuch went to worship God, but he didn't find God there. Instead, what he found was the religious leaders of the day persecuting the followers of Christ (Acts 8:1–3). Those who thought they were insiders with God, for whom there was no obstacle to entry into the earthly temple, were really outsiders—for exactly the same reason the Ethiopian eunuch ultimately became an insider. It is only in Christ that our sins and transgressions can be atoned for and we can stand before a holy God. The prophet Isaiah was called to shout his message out loud to people who thought they were right with God but were actually self-deceived. The reality of their situation was quite different: as Isaiah put it,

> We have all become like one who is unclean,
> and all our righteous deeds are like a polluted garment.
> We all fade like a leaf,
> and our iniquities, like the wind, take us away.
> There is no one who calls upon your name,
> who rouses himself to take hold of you;
> for you have hidden your face from us,
> and have made us melt in the hand of our iniquities.
> (Isa. 64:6–7)

God had actually turned his face away from his people because of their sins, because even their best acts fell far short of his perfect standard. They too needed the acceptance that the Ethiopian eunuch found in Christ. But tragically they never even realized it. The doorway to religion was wide open for them, but they would never find God by entering through that door. They could begin to find a way home only by recognizing that their disfigured hearts excluded them from the reality of God's presence as comprehensively as the eunuch's disfigured flesh excluded him from the outward symbol of God's presence. Only by abandoning trust in their own perfection could they find true hope in the perfection of another.

It may be that you can think of no reasons why God shouldn't welcome you in. Perhaps you have always been a churchgoer, an insider. You grew up in a church family and have always been a good person. You have committed no "great sin" in your life: you've never committed adultery or been divorced or had an abortion. Perhaps you have no concept of what it is to struggle with a life-dominating sin: you've always been a clean-cut, upright citizen. If so, then the gospel that Philip declared to the Ethiopian eunuch challenges you. It tells those who think that they are just fine with God to "get lost." Without Christ's perfection in your place, you are utterly lost before God, no matter how comfortable you feel in church. If your own efforts at goodness could be enough to please God without Jesus, then the cross was a waste of pain and suffering. You too need the kind of conversion experience that the Ethiopian eunuch had so that you can find a genuine welcome with God.

The Joy of the Gospel

Lastly, believer, this passage addresses you as well. First, it says something about your baptism. In our culture, many people view baptism as a testimony about our love for God and our decision to follow him. If that is the case, when, or even if, you get baptized is entirely up to you. Of course, God would be honored to have you as part of his family; the only question is whether you are willing to decide for him. But this views our adoption into Christ entirely the wrong way around. Think about that image of adoption for a moment. Suppose an orphan were to lurk at a freeway rest area waiting for a suitable family to drive through. Then, after watching them happily eating their pizza, as they go back to their car, the orphan joins them and declares himself part of the family. That's not how adoption works: the orphan would be more likely to get arrested for stalking than welcomed in.

Adoption has two parts: the adoptive family chooses you, and then they go to the courthouse and undertake the legal transaction that declares to the world that you belong to them. Becoming a Christian is similar. God adopts us into his family, which means that he chooses us and not we him. We certainly respond to that choice as he opens our eyes to the truth of the gospel. But he takes the initiative in our conversion because only he can invite the outsider in and give the spiritually blind eyes to see and hearts to believe. Then he graciously calls us to baptism, the public declaration on his part that he considers us part of the church. That's why the Ethiopian's baptism was so special to him: it testified that he too had been chosen and included by grace in God's family.

This also explains the covenant baptism of our children in Presbyterian churches like the ones in which I serve. When parents adopt a child, do they wait to file the papers formally bringing the child into the family, until the child is old enough to decide for themselves? Of course not! The child is often legally adopted while still very young so that the adoptive parents can assure them that they really belong to the family as they grow up. So too when we baptize our children, we assure them of their joyful privilege of growing up as children of God. They still need to exercise their own faith in Christ once they are grown, of course. But they start as insiders to God's grace, not outsiders.

So if you haven't been baptized yet, you need to ask yourself the same question that the eunuch asked Philip: "What prevents me from being baptized?" (Acts 8:36). Is it because you are merely stalking the church? If you haven't trusted Christ and his goodness as your hope before God, you are simply hiding among his family, hoping that he won't notice the difference between you and the other kids. Or have you been adopted by God into his family, but you haven't yet received the public affirmation of God that your true status before him is an insider to his grace? If that is the case, then it is time to seek baptism. Can you imagine an orphan not caring about whether they were legally part of their new family or not? Of course they would want to have the whole matter publicly sealed and settled.

Second, do you have the joy that ought to flow from a true understanding of the gospel? Both in Samaria and for the Ethiopian, the acceptance of the gospel brought incredible joy (8:8, 39). Hopelessness became hope, exclusion from God became inclusion into his family. The result was abounding joy. We should have a similar joy, yet it sometimes seems we have mislaid it somewhere along the way. Most likely this is because we have forgotten who we were, who we are, or who we are going to be.

If you've lost your joy, it may be that you have forgotten who you were by nature. You've forgotten that outside of Christ you once had no hope and no future. You were utterly lost and rejected in your transgressions and sins—and that is just as true whether you lived a "good" life outside Christ or whether you were dragged to him kicking and screaming out of the gutter of life. Without Christ, you were utterly dead, whether you presented as a spiritual corpse or a spiritual zombie. Spiritual corpses are irreligious people without Christ. At least corpses are honest enough to act what they are: dead. Spiritual zombies are religious people without

Christ, and they are much scarier: They are just as dead as the spiritual corpses, but they insist on acting as if they are alive. They go to church, they are kind to their neighbors, and they try hard to keep the rules, but they are still dead inside. Don't forget what you once were: lost and without hope in this world before Christ found you.

In Christ, former zombies and former corpses are raised to new life. In Christ you have even now been blessed with every spiritual blessing in the heavenly realms (Eph. 1:3–14). If you are a believer, that is your spiritual identity. You belong to God, and he will not let you go. Even though you still carry around the scars of your former existence, the bitter fruits of your former sinful acts and habits, scars that will haunt you until the day that you die, those scars are not who you are. In Christ you are a new creation. You who once were dead are now alive! God says to you, "Welcome in! Nothing prevents you from coming into my presence, my daughter! Nothing holds you at a distance, my son. Neither your sin nor your flawed righteousness can prevent you from entering my presence and receiving the eternal life that flows from me. Welcome home." Your identity as a believer is a child of the living God and heir of the King of creation.

At the same time, don't forget what you will be one day: whole. The Ethiopian eunuch was not physically healed by Philip. God gave him new life, but not yet a new body. He would have to live with his disability his whole life through. Doubtless he had to live with the emotional scars as well. But he would not be thus forever. One day his disability would be gone: He would have a new body that was whole, complete, perfect. So, too, you and I live day by day with various physical and emotional disabilities; we struggle with painfully broken relationships; we mourn the grinding reality of our sin. Often these things rob us of our joy. We look at our failures as husbands and wives, or as parents and children, and our joy evaporates. We look at our failings as individuals—the besetting sins that we don't tell anyone about, yet which are a daily reality in our lives—and they sap our joy.

Whenever you are confronted afresh with your sin, your guilt is meant to drive you to the cross, where Jesus paid for that sin. That guilt is meant to lift your eyes to heaven, where you will be healed from that sin. Our hearts are not yet whole; our bodies are not yet restored; our spirits are not yet made perfect. But one day they will be. The prophet Isaiah foresaw that too: the Lord says,

> For behold, I create new heavens
>   and a new earth,
> and the former things shall not be remembered
>   or come into mind.
> But be glad and rejoice forever
>   in that which I create;
> for behold, I create Jerusalem to be a joy,
>   and her people to be a gladness.
> I will rejoice in Jerusalem
>   and be glad in my people;
> no more shall be heard in it the sound of weeping
>   and the cry of distress. (Isa. 65:17–19)

That picture of heavenly glory should fill your heart with joy, as it surely did for the Ethiopian eunuch as he read on in the Isaiah scroll he had purchased. God promises not only a new heavens and a new earth but, best of all, a new me and a new you in whom God himself will take delight forever. He promises to bring to completion the work of sanctification that he has already begun in us (Phil. 1:6). He shows us an eternal welcome for the people of God into his presence, paid for and assured by the price paid by the suffering servant, Jesus. There we will join the Ethiopian eunuch in rejoicing with great joy.

I pray that something of that heavenly joy touches your heart and soul even now. I pray that this joy spills over from you into the lives of those around you so they too will become fellow worshipers of the risen Christ.

General Index

Scripture Index

Also Available from Iain Duguid

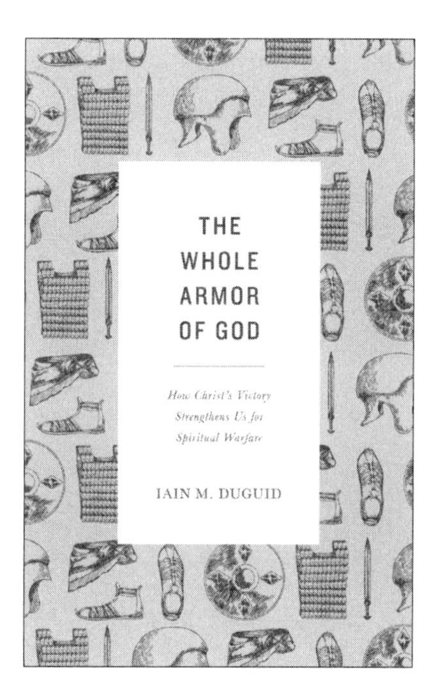

Duguid walks through the "armor of God" passage in Ephesians, examining the Old Testament context of each piece of armor and encouraging readers as they fight sin while resting in the finished victory of Christ.

For more information, visit **crossway.org**.